CU00650646

STEP NOTES

HEALTH AND SAFETY LAW

Contents

Health and Safety Law Step Notes

Contents

Contents

Contents

INTRODUCTION

◆ What do you understand by absolute and qualified duties?

◆ How does the appeals procedure work in a criminal case?

◆ What are the responsibilities of the "responsible person" under the **Regulatory Reform (Fire Safety) Order**?

As a Health and Safety Adviser, you need to have a good understanding of legal fundamentals. If you are already working in health and safety, you will be familiar with many legal issues. But these short notes have been compiled to define basic legal terms and terms you may come across in your work or studies.

A

ABSOLUTE AND QUALIFIED DUTIES

Failing to meet the statutory duties laid down in health and safety legislation may give rise to criminal action.

Certain duties under health and safety law are of an absolute nature and must be complied with regardless of cost, practicability, etc. They are accompanied by the terms "shall" or "must"; the word 'practicable' will be absent. An example is the duty of employers to conduct risk assessments under the **Management of Health and Safety at Work Regulations, Regulation 3(1)**, whereby:

> *"Every employer shall make a suitable and sufficient assessment of ... the risks to the health and safety of his employees to which they are exposed whilst they are at work;....."*

There are three distinct levels of duty: absolute, practicable and reasonably practicable.

◆ **Absolute requirements**, e.g. where the risk of injury or disease is inevitable if requirements are not followed (see *Summers v. Frost (1955)* in the Appendix).

For example: **Regulation 4, Provision and Use of Work Equipment Regulations 1998:** Every employer **shall** ensure that work equipment is so constructed or adapted as to be suitable for the purpose for which it is used or provided.

◆ **Practicable requirements** - imply that if, in the light of current knowledge and invention, it is feasible to comply with these requirements, irrespective of cost or sacrifice, then such requirements must be complied with (*Schwalb v. Fass H. & Son (1946)*).

Practicable means more than physically possible and implies a higher duty of care than a duty qualified by **so far as is reasonably practicable**. This level of legal duty effectively obliges employers to keep abreast of, and install if necessary, up-to-the-minute technology to overcome problems regardless of cost but does not impose a duty to invent solutions if they are not already in existence (see *Adsett v. K&L Steelfounders & Engineers Ltd (1953)* in the Appendix).

◆ **Reasonably practicable requirements** - imply a lower or lesser level of duty.

Reasonably practicable is a narrower term than physically possible and implies that a computation must be made in which the quantum of risk is placed on one side of the scale and the sacrifice involved in carrying out the measures necessary for averting the risk is placed on the other side (see *Edwards v. National Coal Board (1949)* in the Appendix).

© RRC International

If it can be shown that there is gross disproportion between the above factors, i.e. the risk is insignificant in relation to the sacrifice, then a defendant discharges the onus on themselves (*Edwards v. National Coal Board (1949)*). In essence, therefore, the duty holder need only balance cost against risk in cases where the duty is qualified by the phrase 'so far as is reasonably practicable.'

ACAS

The Advisory, Conciliation and Arbitration Service (ACAS) was established by the **Employment Protection Act 1975 (EPA)** (now consolidated into the Employment **Rights Act 1996 (ERA)**).

The functions of ACAS are:

◆ To advise employers and trade unions on any matter concerned with employment policies and industrial relations.

◆ To conciliate in matters such as maternity leave, trade union membership and activities, dismissals and redundancies.

◆ To arbitrate, at the request of both parties.

ACAS has a general duty to promote good industrial/employee relations and to encourage the extension of collective bargaining.

Conciliation is undertaken through a Conciliation Officer who endeavours to reach a settlement before the case goes to an employment tribunal.

Arbitration, with the consent of all parties, follows unsuccessful conciliation and can be through an independent arbitrator or the Central Arbitration Committee.

ACAS gives advice in the following areas to employers, employees and their representative bodies:

◆ Organisation of workers for collective bargaining purposes.

◆ Recognition of trade unions by employers.

◆ Negotiating machinery and joint consultation.

◆ Disputes and grievance procedures.

◆ Communications between employers and employees.

◆ Facilities and time off for trade union officials.

◆ Procedures relating to termination of employment.

◆ Disciplinary matters.

- Staff planning, labour turnover and absenteeism.

- Recruitment, retention, promotion and vocational training.

- Payment systems, equal pay, equal value and job evaluation.

The Central Arbitration Committee (CAC) was established by the **EPA 1975** (now in **ERA 1996**) and consists of a chairperson, deputy chairperson, and a panel of persons representing employers and employees, appointed by the Secretary of State after consultation with ACAS.

Though independent of ACAS, the CAC deals with matters referred to it by ACAS, in particular complaints regarding employers who refuse to disclose information required by law, matters relating to payment of wages, amendments to collective agreements, pay structures or wages orders, and disputes within a statutory joint industrial council.

ACCESS TO INFORMATION FOR CIVIL ACTIONS

Where an employee is suing an employer he will need access to certain information.

Under Section 28 of the **Health and Safety at Work, etc. Act 1974 (HSWA)**, as amended by the **Employment Protection Act 1975**, anyone involved in civil proceedings may obtain from the HSE a written statement of relevant factual information obtained by an Inspector in the exercise of his powers.

This is usually applied for by a solicitor.

APPEALS PROCEDURE - CRIMINAL COURTS

Where a person is convicted of a summary offence there is right of appeal to a Crown Court against:

- Conviction, sentence or both, if the accused pleaded not guilty.

- Sentence only if he pleaded guilty.

Appeals from the Crown Court are heard by the Court of Appeal, Criminal Division.

Both prosecution and defendant may appeal on a point of law by way of case stated to the High Court (Divisional Court of the Queen's Bench Division). The lower court states a case for the High Court to adjudicate on.

APPROVED CODES OF PRACTICE (ACOPS)

Section 16 of the **Health and Safety at Work, etc. Act 1974 (HSWA)** gives the HSE power to prepare and approve codes of practice on matters contained not only in regulations, but in Sections 2-7 of **HSWA**.

© RRC International

The HSE must consult with any interested body prior to approving a code.

An ACoP is a **quasi-legal document**; non-compliance does not constitute a breach of law.

Where a breach of **HSWA** or regulations is alleged, the fact that an ACoP was not followed could be accepted as evidence of failure to do all that was reasonably practicable.

A defence of having carried out works of equivalent nature can be offered as an alternative to compliance with an ACoP.

ACoPs give advice on how to comply with the law by, for example, providing an explanation of what is "reasonably practicable". For example, if regulations use words like "suitable and sufficient", an ACoP can illustrate what this requires in particular circumstances.

B

BRITISH, EUROPEAN AND INTERNATIONAL STANDARDS

The British Standards Institution (BSI) produces safety standards and codes through committees formed to deal with a specific matter or subject, such as machinery safety.

Standards contain details relating to, for instance, the construction of and materials incorporated in an item and, where necessary, prescribe methods of testing to establish compliance.

Codes deal with safe working practices and systems of work.

British Standards and Codes have no legal status, but can be interpreted by the courts as being the authoritative guidance on a particular matter.

Many British Standards are now being superseded by EU Standards denoted by the "CE" mark on various goods, etc. Many regulations now require that equipment must comply with EU standards, e.g. the **Provision and Use of Work Equipment Regulations 1998**, the **Personal Protective Equipment (PPE) at Work Regulations 1992**, as amended, and various safety regulations relating to particular products.

Some British Standards are prefixed BS EN ISO indicating that they qualify also as European or International Standards.

National Standards

British Standards all carry the prefix BS.

Published Documents (PDs) is a catch-all category for standards-type documents that do not have the same status as a BS. Some PDs are adoptions of CEN (Comité Européen de Normalisation), CENELEC (Comité Européen de Normalisation Electrotechnique), ISO (International Organisation for Standardisation) or IEC (International Electrotechnical Commission) publications.

A **Publicly Available Specification** (PAS) is a standard developed by BSI commissioned by an external organisation. Such external bodies have included the UK Government, trade associations and private companies.

Adopted Publications - International

As a member of ISO and IEC, BSI has the option of adopting any international standard as a British Standard.

© RRC International

Adopted Publications - European

As a member of CEN and CENELEC, BSI is obliged to adopt all European Standards and to withdraw any national standards that might conflict with them.

BUILDING REGULATIONS 2010 (SI 2010 NO. 2214)

The **Building Regulations** set out the procedures needed to obtain approval for certain kinds of building work and the technical requirements of such work. The main area where the **Building Regulations** affect health and safety is in fire safety.

The **Building Regulations** 2010 came into force in October 2010 and revoked the previous 2000 regulations. The changes related principally to energy conservation and had little impact on fire safety.

In general, the **Building Regulations** impose requirements on people carrying out building work and contain provisions directed at:

◆ Securing the safety, health, welfare and convenience of persons in and about buildings.

◆ Furthering the conservation of fuel and power.

◆ Preventing waste and contamination of water.

Requirements to limit fire deal with:

◆ Internal fire spread on walls and ceilings and within the structure.

◆ External fire spread through walls and roofs.

◆ Specific requirements for dwellings, flats, offices and stairways.

There must be appropriate provision for early warning and a means of escape in case of fire from within a building to a place of safety outside the building, and reference must be made, in such cases, to Mandatory Rules for Means of Escape in Case of Fire.

There must be ample air space for people in buildings.

Stairways must be properly guarded and, where appropriate, fitted with handrails.

Roofs, roof lights and balconies to which people have access for purposes other than normal maintenance and repair must be guarded.

Stairways and ramps must be constructed in such a way that they afford safe passage to people using them.

Practical guidance on ways to comply with the functional requirements in the **Building Regulations** is outlined in a series of "Approved Documents" published by the Department for Communities and Local Government.

Each document contains:

◆ General guidance on the performance expected of materials and building work in order to comply with each of the requirements of the **Building Regulations**.

◆ Practical examples and solutions on how to achieve compliance for some of the more common building situations.

The Approved Documents of specific relevance to fire safety are:

◆ *The Building Regulations 2010 Approved Document B - Fire Safety, Volume 2: Buildings other than dwelling houses.*

◆ *The Building Regulations 2010 Approved Document M - Access to and use of buildings: Volume 2 - Buildings other than dwellings.*

BURDEN AND ONUS OF PROOF

Burden of Proof

Criminal law generally requires the prosecution to prove "**beyond all reasonable doubt**" that a person has committed an offence. This does not have to mean 'absolute certainty' but merely that those deciding upon guilt are 'sure' that the accused has committed an offence.

The burden of proof in a **civil case** is less onerous and is termed "**on the balance of probabilities**". Those deciding on liability (usually a judge) will simply need to prefer one version of events over the other.

Onus of Proof

In a **criminal case**, the onus of proof is generally on the prosecution to prove that the accused has committed an offence (there is a presumption of innocence). However, under S.40 of the **Health and Safety at Work, etc. Act 1974**, the onus rests on the accused to prove that it was not practicable or reasonably practicable to satisfy the duty or requirement. In a trial for a breach of **HSWA** and/or Regulations, the prosecution need only prove that a breach of the Act and/or Regulations took place, and that the accused was responsible for breaching the law.

In a **civil case**, the onus is on the claimant to make his or her case.

© RRC International

C

CARRIAGE OF DANGEROUS GOODS AND USE OF TRANSPORTABLE PRESSURE EQUIPMENT REGULATIONS 2009 (SI 2009 NO. 1348)

This is a very technical piece of legislation but much of the technical detail is hidden. This is because it makes reference to **ADR** (the European Agreement concerning the International Carriage of Dangerous Goods by Road) and RID (the Regulations concerning the International Carriage of Dangerous Goods by Rail). **ADR** and **RID** deal with the carriage of dangerous goods (such as corrosives, flammables) by road and rail respectively across Europe. There is also a brief mention of carriage of dangerous goods by inland waterways, but only in relation to safety advisers.

The Regulations are split up into seven parts:

◆ Introductory Provisions;

◆ Prohibitions and Requirements;

◆ Exemptions;

◆ Transportable Pressure Equipment;

◆ Radiological Emergencies;

◆ GB Competent Authority Functions;

◆ Miscellaneous;

and three schedules.

The Regulations also require (by reference to **ADR**) employers who transport dangerous goods to appoint a vocationally qualified safety adviser (usually called a 'Dangerous Goods Safety Adviser'). The basic principles are:

◆ The number and source (i.e. employee or consultant) of safety advisers is for employers to decide.

◆ Safety advisers must hold a vocational training certificate valid for modes of transport used and types of dangerous goods carried.

◆ Certificates are valid for five years, after which refresher examinations must be taken.

Some of the main duties of Dangerous Goods Safety Advisers are to:

◆ Monitor legal compliance requirements on the transport of dangerous goods.

◆ Prepare accident reports.

◆ Assist the employer on health, safety and environmental matters.

◆ Prepare annual reports summarising monitoring activities.

Some exceptions apply to:

◆ Recipients of dangerous goods.

◆ Employers who handle small quantities of some dangerous goods.

In relation to road transport of dangerous goods as liquids or gases in bulk, the following terms are frequently distinguished:

◆ **Road tanker** means a goods vehicle which has a tank which is an integral part of the vehicle or is attached to the frame of the vehicle and is not intended to be removed from it.

◆ **Tank container** means a tank, whether or not subdivided into separate compartments, with a total capacity of more than 450 litres and includes a tube container and a tank swap body.

◆ **Tube container** means a group of gas cylinders connected together with a total capacity of more than 450 litres fitted into a framework suitable for lifting on or off a vehicle and intended to be used for the carriage of **compressed gases**.

◆ **Tank swap body** means a tank specially designed for carriage by rail and road only and is without stacking capability.

Vehicles and tanks must be properly designed and of adequate strength and construction to convey dangerous substances by road.

The operator is responsible for:

◆ Ensuring that the regulations on the conveyance of certain substances are enforced and that tanks are not overfilled.

◆ Giving written information, or 'Instructions in Writing' (formerly known as Transport Emergency Cards, or 'TREm Cards') to drivers on hazards associated with their loads and necessary emergency procedures.

© RRC International

The driver must ensure:

◆ The safe parking and supervision of the vehicle when not in use, when prescribed substances are carried.

◆ Precautions to prevent fire or explosion are observed.

All **road tankers** and **tank containers** must display information about the hazardous contents using a system of placards, orange plates and information panels. In the UK, this is brought together in something commonly called a HazChem panel, containing the following information:

◆ Emergency action code (used by UK fire service to communicate fire-fighting measures).

◆ UN number (this identifies the substance or substance type).

◆ Telephone number for specialist advice.

◆ Placard (this is a large hazard warning diamond describing the hazard class of the substance being carried).

'HazChem' panels are not recognised in the rest of the EU. For transport in the EU a different design of panel bearing a 'Kemler Code' (ADR Hazard Identification Number) is used.

CASE LAW

Case law is based on the doctrine of judicial precedent and its principles and doctrines are to be found in the law reports, e.g. All England Reports (AER). It is a self-endorsing process, perpetuated either by previous binding cases or by the interpretation of legislation.

The following features of a judgment are important:

◆ *Ratio decidendi* (reason for the decision) - a statement of law based on an examination of the facts and the legal issues surrounding them. This is the most important part of a judgment and contains the actual binding precedent.

◆ *Obiter dicta* (words said by the way) - may contain a statement about the law which is not based on the facts of the case under review and which will not therefore be part of the decision. This is often held to be of persuasive authority.

(See the Appendix for an outline of some key health and safety law cases.)

CENTRAL ARBITRATION COMMITTEE

(See under **ACAS**.)

CIVIL COURT PROCEDURE

Most civil proceedings are heard by a judge sitting alone.

The report by Lord Woolf, the then Master of the Rolls, entitled *Access to Justice* altered the procedure for bringing civil actions and applies to proceedings commenced on or after 24 April 1999. Terminology also changed, in an apparent effort to make the system easier to understand. The 'Plaintiff' is now known as the 'Claimant,' an 'Affidavit' is now called a 'Witness statement,' and a 'Writ' is now known as a 'Claim form'.

The main aims of this revised system were to:

◆ Enable courts to deal with cases justly.

◆ Speed up and simplify the civil litigation process.

◆ Reduce/make proportionate legal costs.

◆ Reduce the adversarial approach.

◆ Reduce the amount of litigation.

One key concept was the introduction of 'Pre-action protocols'. These aim to:

◆ Enhance pre-litigation contact.

◆ Ensure exchange of information.

◆ Help pre-litigation investigation.

◆ Reduce the need for litigation.

◆ Speed up the post-litigation timetable.

◆ Reduce costs.

Strict timescales were also introduced.

The first stage in proceedings is the issue of a 'Letter of claim' (known previously as a 'Writ'). The defendant is given 21 days to reply to a letter of claim and there is a 13-week deadline for liability response, at which time full document disclosure must take place. Examples of documents to be disclosed might include, but should not be limited to, the accident book entry, the accident investigation report, earnings information, minutes of the health and safety committee meetings, training records, risk assessments, safe systems of work and machinery maintenance logs.

© RRC International

For relatively straightforward matters, the trial is to take place no more than 30 weeks after issue of Directions.

Experts are instructed jointly by agreement between both sides. Their duty is to the Court. There are restrictions on evidence (particularly verbal evidence) and there is a set format for expert reports.

Claims are placed on one of three 'tracks' roughly according to the size of the claim, though this does not always follow.

◆ Small Claims:

> ▸ Property: £10,000 or less.

> ▸ Personal injury: £1,000 or less.

◆ Fast Track:

> ▸ For proceedings issued on or after 6 April 2009, of not more than £25,000.

> ▸ For proceedings issued before 6 April 2009, of not more than £15,000.

> ▸ Multi Track: normal track for any claim for which the Small Claims track or the Fast Track is not the normal track.

CIVIL LIABILITY

This refers to the sanction (or 'penalty') that can be imposed by a civil court.

A civil action generally involves individuals, with a claimant suing a defendant for a remedy or remedies. In most cases the remedy takes the form of damages, a form of financial compensation.

A civil case must be proved on the balance of probabilities, which is a lesser standard than that of beyond reasonable doubt required in a criminal case.

Many claims for injuries sustained at work pass through the civil courts or may be settled out of court. Actions may be for negligence or breach of contract.

The civil courts are the County Court and the High Court.

Civil Liability - Breach of Statutory Duty

Where an accident occurred before 1 October 2013, it used to be the case that a breach of criminal duty imposed by a statute or regulations gave rise to civil liability and a claim for damages.

The standard test adopted by the courts was to ask the question:

"Was the duty imposed specifically for the protection of a particular class of person, or was it intended to benefit the public at large?"

If the answer to the first part of the question was "yes", a civil claim may be allowed subject to the following conditions:

◆ the claimant must be a member of the above class; and

◆ there must have been breach of the statute or regulation; and

◆ the claimant must have suffered damage of a kind against which the statute/regulation was designed to give protection; and

◆ the claimant's damage must actually have been caused by the breach of statutory duty.

However, since the coming into force of Section 69 of the **Enterprise and Regulatory Reform Act 2013** on 1 October 2013, there have been significant changes to a claimant's approach to civil actions against an employer for health and safety breaches. Prior to the change, S.47(2) of the **Health and Safety at Work, etc. Act 1974 (HSWA)** conferred a civil right of action unless the Regulations expressly provided otherwise. Section 69 of the 2013 Act amends Section 47 of **HSWA** to require that there should be **no** civil right of action for breach of a duty imposed by certain health and safety legislation, other than where such a right is specifically provided for. Claimants will now need to show that an employer has been negligent under the common law rules of tort and employers will no longer be strictly liable for civil claims for breach of health and safety duties set out in legislation.

An exception to this arises from the **Health and Safety at Work etc. Act 1974 (Civil Liability) (Exceptions) Regulations 2013,** which aim to ensure that a pregnant worker continues to have the right to bring a claim for breach of statutory health and safety duty in relation to rights under the **Pregnant Workers Directive.** The **Management of Health and Safety at Work Regulations 1999** have been amended to allow new or expectant mothers to bring a civil claim for breach of those Regulations which impose specific duties on employers in relation to such employees.

CLASSIFICATION, LABELLING AND PACKAGING REGULATION (CLP) (EC REGULATION 1272/2008)

This European Regulation is directly binding on member states. It has been phased in to implement the Globally Harmonised System (GHS) of classification and labelling and has now replaced the British **CHIP Regulations.**

The European Commission has designed the **CLP Regulation** to fit in with the **Regulation on the Registration, Evaluation, Authorisation and Restriction of Chemicals (REACH)** that came into force in June 2007.

© RRC International

CLP sets out rules for the classification of substances and mixtures. Before a substance or mixture is marketed, the supplier must classify it in respect of physical, health and environmental hazards.

Physical hazards include explosives, flammable liquids, flammable gases, flammable aerosols, flammable solids, etc.

There are ten different health hazards, some subdivided into categories, e.g. acute toxicity categories 1, 2, 3 and 4.

Environmental hazards include hazardous to the aquatic environment and hazardous to the ozone layer.

Containers of hazardous substances and mixtures must be labelled in order to communicate information on the hazards to users. Harmonised warning and precautionary statements must be placed on labels as well as warning pictograms.

Hazard statements describe the nature of the hazards associated with the chemical, and where appropriate the degree of hazard, e.g. "H220: Extremely flammable gas".

Precautionary statements describe recommended measures to minimise or prevent adverse effects resulting from exposure to a hazardous substance or mixture due to its use or disposal, e.g. "P210: Keep away from heat/sparks/open flames/hot surfaces. - No smoking"; "P403: Store in a well-ventilated place."

There are nine pictograms introduced for labels. These are a red diamond-shaped outline, with black drawing on a white background.

COMMON LAW

This is a body of accumulated case law (both criminal and civil) which is based on the decisions of the courts over many years whereby precedents are established.

◆ **Binding (or 'Authoritative') precedents** are of universal application and must be followed by all courts below that which set the precedent. Until recently, this included the Supreme Court (formerly the appellate committee of the House of Lords), though they may now overrule a previous decision of their own in favour of one which, for example, more closely matches the prevailing policy considerations.

◆ Precedents are recorded in the various Law Reports, e.g. the All England Reports (AER).

◆ **Persuasive precedents** are decisions which are not binding upon a court, but which a judge may take into consideration (e.g. Commonwealth and USA cases, etc.).

    Applicable to decisions made by courts at their own level and from superior courts.

COMPETENT PERSONS

Regulation 7 of the Management of Health and Safety at Work Regulations 1999, as amended, defines a competent person as "a person who has sufficient training and experience or knowledge and other qualities" to assist the employer in compliance with legislation.

Case law *(Brazier v. Skipton Rock Co. Ltd (1962))* defines a competent person as one with practical and theoretical knowledge as well as sufficient experience of the particular machinery, plant or procedure involved to enable him to identify defects or weaknesses during plant and machinery examinations, and to assess their importance in relation to the strength and function of that plant and machinery.

Competent persons must be appointed for the following construction-related activities:

◆ Supervision of demolition work.

◆ Supervision of the handling and use of explosives.

◆ Inspection of scaffold materials prior to erection of a scaffold.

◆ Supervision or erection of, substantial alterations or additions to, and dismantling of, scaffolds.

◆ Inspection of scaffolds at regular intervals not exceeding seven days and after adverse weather conditions.

◆ Inspection of excavations before any person carries out work at the start of every shift.

◆ Supervision of the erection of cranes.

◆ Testing of cranes after erection, re-erection and any removal or adjustment involving changes of anchorage or ballasting.

◆ Examination of appliances for anchorage or ballasting prior to crane erection.

The requirement to use competent persons is commonplace in legislation. Here are some further examples where their use is mandated:

◆ Examination of lifting equipment (which includes chains, ropes, lifting tackle, new lifting machines and power-driven lifts, etc.) and examination and testing of lifting appliances and lifting gear (**Lifting Operations and Lifting Equipment Regulations 1998**).

◆ Mounting of abrasive wheels, etc. (**Provision and Use of Work Equipment Regulations 1998**).

© RRC International

◆ Noise assessments (**Control of Noise at Work Regulations 2005**).

◆ Preparation of written schemes of examination (**Pressure Systems Safety Regulations 2000**).

◆ Assisting employers in undertaking measures to comply with requirements and prohibitions imposed by or under the relevant statutory provisions (**Management of Health and Safety at Work Regulations 1999**).

◆ Persons must be competent to prevent danger and injury (e.g. **Electricity at Work Regulations 1989**, Regulation 16), etc.

CONFINED SPACES REGULATIONS 1997 (SI 1997 NO. 1713)

The **Confined Spaces Regulations 1997** apply to confined spaces in all parts of industry, defined as any place such as a tank, pit, sewer or well in which, by virtue of its enclosed nature, there arises a reasonably foreseeable specified risk.

The **specified risks** covered include fire or explosion; loss of consciousness from hyperthermia; asphyxiation from gas, fume, vapour, free flowing solid or lack of oxygen; and drowning in a liquid. A congested area is not a confined space unless at least one of the foregoing risks is present.

The Regulations require the full implementation of risk assessments including safe systems of work, i.e. avoidance of entry if possible; permit-to-work operation; and provision of adequate rescue and resuscitation arrangements.

CONSTRUCTION (DESIGN AND MANAGEMENT) REGULATIONS 2015 (CDM) (SI 2015 NO. 51)

These replace similarly named regulations from 2007.

They place general and specific duties on clients, designers, principal designers, principal contractors, other contractors and workers.

The Regulations are divided into five parts.

◆ Part 1 deals with matters of interpretation and application.

◆ Part 2 covers **client duties** in relation to managing projects, appointment of the **principal designer** and the **principal contractor,** notification, and application to domestic clients.

◆ Part 3 sets out health and safety duties and roles relating to **designers**, **principal designers**, the **construction phase plan** and **health and safety file**, **principal contractors** and **contractors**.

◆ Part 4 sets out **general requirements for all construction sites** and covers physical safeguards which need to be provided to prevent danger.

◆ Part 5 is concerned with **general** issues such as enforcement in respect of fire and transitional provisions for existing projects.

There are also Schedules to the Regulations that deal with notification, welfare facilities, work involving particular risks and transitional provisions.

Part 1

A **client** is any person for whom a construction project is carried out. One of the key policy changes from the 2007 Regulations is the inclusion of domestic clients. The client's role as head of the supply chain has been recognised, leading to a more central role when compared to the 2007 Regulations.

Contractor means any person (including a non-domestic client) who, in the course or furtherance of a business, carries out, manages or controls construction work.

Designer means any person who carries on a trade or business in connection with which he:

◆ prepares or modifies a design for construction work; or

◆ arranges for or instructs his employee or any person under his control to do so.

Part 2

A client must make suitable arrangements for managing a project, including the allocation of sufficient time and other resources.

The client is required to appoint a **principal designer** and a **principal contractor.**

Projects above the **notification** threshold (projects lasting more than 30 days and involving more than 20 workers at any one time, or involving more than 500 person-days of construction work) are to be notified to the HSE in writing (a form F10 is available). Details of what is to be notified are in Schedule 1 of **CDM 2015**.

The extent to which **domestic clients** must carry out the client duties in **CDM 2015** is limited and most of the duties are passed to other duty holders, most notably the contractor/principal contractor.

Part 3

The **principal designer** is responsible for managing the pre-construction phase of the project.

The **principal contractor** is responsible for managing the construction phase of the project.

© RRC International

Construction Phase Plan

This provides the health and safety focus for the construction phase of the project.

A pre-tender information pack should be prepared by the principal designer in time to make it available to contractors who are tendering or making arrangements to carry out or manage construction work. This should contain the following information:

◆ The project, such as the client brief and key dates of the construction phase.

◆ The planning and management of the project, such as:

   ▸ Resources and time being allocated to each stage of the project.

   ▸ Arrangements to ensure there is co-operation between duty holders and that the work is co-ordinated.

◆ The health and safety hazards of the site, including design and construction hazards.

◆ How health and safety hazards will be addressed.

◆ Any relevant information in an existing health and safety file.

Once appointed, the principal contractor (or contractor if the project involves only one contractor) is responsible for developing the construction phase plan, updating it and monitoring its implementation. This should contain the following information:

◆ Description of the project such as key dates and details of key members of the project team.

◆ Management of the work, including:

   ▸ Health and safety aims for the project.

   ▸ Site rules.

   ▸ Arrangements to ensure co-operation between project team members and co-ordination of their work, such as regular site meetings.

   ▸ Arrangements for involving workers.

   ▸ Site induction.

   ▸ Welfare facilities.

   ▸ Fire and emergency procedures.

◆ Control of any particular risks where they are relevant to the work involved.

It is the responsibility of the client to ensure that the principal contractor has prepared a suitable construction phase plan prior to the commencement of construction work.

The Health and Safety File

This is a record of information which tells the client/end user (or others who might be responsible for the structure in the future) about the key health and safety risks that have to be managed during maintenance, repair or renovation.

The principal designer has to ensure that it is prepared as the project progresses and that it is handed over to the client when the project is complete. The client has to make the file available to those who will work on any future design, building, maintenance or demolition of the structure. If the structure is sold, the client must give the file to the new owner.

The file should include drawings, construction method details, equipment and maintenance facilities, maintenance procedures and requirements for the structure, operation and maintenance manuals and details of utilities, services, emergency and fire-fighting systems.

Part 4

Duties to achieve the standards here are held by contractors who actually carry out the work. Duties are also held by those who do not do construction work themselves, but control the way in which the work is done. In each case, the extent of the duty is in proportion to the degree of control which the individual or organisation has over the work in question.

The specific topics are: safe places of construction work; good order and site security; stability of structures; demolition or dismantling; explosives; excavations; cofferdams and caissons; reports of inspections; energy distribution installations; prevention of drowning; traffic routes; vehicles; prevention of risk from fire, flooding or asphyxiation; emergency procedures; emergency routes and exits; fire detection and fire-fighting; fresh air; temperature and weather protection; and lighting.

Guidance on the Regulations, L153 *Managing Health and Safety in Construction*, gives a more extensive account of the requirements of **CDM 2015**.

CONSTRUCTION REGULATIONS

While most health and safety legislation will apply equally to all workplaces, a number of regulations are of particular relevance to construction activities, notably (see separate entries):

◆ Construction (Design and Management) Regulations 2015.

◆ Control of Asbestos Regulations 2012.

◆ Confined Spaces Regulations 1997.

© RRC International

◆ Lifting Operations and Lifting Equipment Regulations 1998.

◆ Work at Height Regulations 2005.

CONSUMER PROTECTION ACT 1987 (CPA)

Part I of the CPA deals with product liability, making a producer strictly liable for a defective product.

An injured person does not have to show negligence on the part of the producer, but only that the product did not provide the level of safety he or she was entitled to expect.

Producer in relation to a product means the person who manufactured it, or the person who won or abstracted it, or the person who carried out a process to produce that product.

Product means any goods or electricity, and includes a product which is comprised in another product whether by virtue of being a component part or raw material or otherwise.

Liability for a defective product extends to the producer, and/or the person who by branding or putting his name on the product, holds himself to be the producer, and the importer.

Defective implies that the safety of the product is not such as persons are generally entitled to expect, and for those purposes safety in relation to a product shall include safety with respect to products comprised in that product and safety in the context of risks of damage to property, as well as in the context of risks of death or personal injury.

In any civil proceedings, the following defences are open to a producer:

◆ The defect is attributable to compliance with any requirement imposed under any enactment or with any EU obligation.

◆ The person did not at any time supply the product.

◆ That the following conditions are satisfied:

   ‣ That the only supply of the product to another was otherwise than in the course of a business to that person.

   ‣ That it does not apply to the person by virtue of things done otherwise than with a view to profit.

◆ That the defect did not exist in the product at the relevant time.

◆ That the state of scientific and technical knowledge at the relevant time was not such that the producer might have been expected to discover the defect.

Damage means death or personal injury or any loss of or damage to any property (including land). Any damage for which a person is liable shall be deemed to have been caused:

◆ For the purposes of the **Fatal Accidents Act 1976**, by that person's wrongful act, neglect or default.

◆ For the purposes of the **Law Reform (Miscellaneous Provisions) (Scotland) Act 1940**, by that person's wrongful act or negligent act or omission.

◆ For the purposes of the **Damages (Scotland) Act 1976**, by that person's act or omission.

CONTRACT LAW

A contract is a legally binding agreement backed by consideration between two parties with contractual capacity.

It consists of an offer made by one party that must be accepted by the other.

There must be consideration that flows from the first party to the second party and vice versa. In this context, 'Consideration' is the thing of value offered in exchange for goods and/or services. Examples include goods for money, work for pay, accommodation for rent, etc.

There must be intention, whereby the parties concerned must intend to enter into a legally binding agreement.

Both parties must have legal capacity, i.e. be sane (i.e. not a 'Patient' within the meaning of the **Mental Health Acts**), sober and 18 years of age or older.

Certain other essentials have to be complied with.

CONTRACT OF EMPLOYMENT

This is fundamentally a contract between employer and employee, which follows:

◆ An offer of a job which is accepted.

◆ Terms of employment, which are express (stated verbally and/or in writing), implied (e.g. by custom and practice), and may be incorporated (through collective bargaining agreements).

Under the **Employment Rights Act 1996 (ERA)** the contract must incorporate a written statement of main particulars specifying parties to the contract, date of employment,

© RRC International

rate of payment, hours of work, benefits, job title, length of notice and other conditions. Subsequent legislative amendments require that every employee (including part-time workers) is given a written statement of the main terms of their contract within two months of beginning work.

Statutory constraints must be considered by an employer, such as pay, as laid down in the **Equal Pay Act 1970** and the **National Minimum Wage Act 1998**; benefits (e.g. statutory sick pay, etc.); and working conditions (e.g. **Working Time Regulations 1998**).

Other statutes must also be complied with, e.g.:

◆ **Equality Act 2010**.

◆ **Trade Union and Labour Relations (Consolidation) Act 1992**.

◆ **Trade Union Reform and Employment Rights Act 1993**.

Provision for variation of contract may be incorporated in a contract of employment. If this is not included, variations must be by mutual agreement.

CONTRACTORS

A contractor is one who is engaged to perform a certain task without direction from the person employing him or her. Note the distinction between an independent contractor engaged to perform a specific task, and an employee (or servant) who can be directed in terms of how to undertake a task.

The basic test of whether a person is an independent contractor is one of control over the undertaking of the work.

Independent contractors working in another person's workplace are, in the main, responsible for their torts and those of their servants, i.e. employees.

An occupier or employer must be careful in selecting a reliable independent contractor, i.e. one who is competent to perform the task required and who employs skilled and competent workers.

An occupier cannot escape liability by putting out a job to a contractor which he, the occupier, has a statutory duty to perform.

Special definitions are contained in some Regulations (e.g. see earlier **CDM Regulations**).

CONTROL OF ARTIFICIAL OPTICAL RADIATION AT WORK REGULATIONS 2010 (SI 2010 NO. 1140)

Employers are required to identify any artificial light sources that could cause harm, e.g. from welding, furnaces or UV curing of prints. Where such hazardous light sources are used, the employer must implement control measures to reduce the risk of harm to eyes and skin of employees to as low as is reasonably practicable. Where there are five or more employees, it should be recorded in a risk assessment.

CONTROL OF ASBESTOS REGULATIONS 2012 AS AMENDED (SI 2012 NO. 632)

Asbestos is an example of a dangerous substance which enters the body via the respiratory system. There are at least six types of asbestos, including the commonly used blue, brown or white (although the colour is not indicative of its relative danger). Import, supply or use of asbestos is strictly prohibited in the UK. It may still be found in buildings as a heat and noise insulator; it may also be found in fire protection materials. Any new product containing asbestos must carry warning labels.

The **Control of Asbestos Regulations 2012** update the previous **Control of Asbestos Regulations 2006** which consolidated legislation on the prohibition of asbestos, the control of asbestos at work and asbestos licensing. The 2012 Asbestos Regulations address the European Commission's view that the UK had not fully implemented the EU Directive on exposure to asbestos (**Directive 2009/148/EC**) by taking into account work carried out on materials that might release fibres when disturbed (friable) or deteriorate once worked on. Under the previous regulations this would be classed as non-licensed work but the new regulations introduce the new category of Notifiable Non-Licensed Work. In practice the changes are limited to requiring some types of non-licensed work with asbestos to be notified to the appropriate enforcing authority and for such work to involve medical surveillance and records kept of exposure.

The importation, supply and use of all forms of asbestos is prohibited, as is the second-hand use of asbestos products such as asbestos cement sheets and asbestos boards and tiles, including panels which have been covered with paint or textured plaster containing asbestos.

If existing asbestos-containing materials are in good condition, they may be left in place, their condition monitored and managed to ensure they are not disturbed.

The **Control of Asbestos Regulations** include the 'duty to manage asbestos' in non-domestic premises. Guidance on the duty to manage asbestos can be found in the Approved Code of Practice L143 *Managing and working with asbestos*.

© RRC International

The Regulations require mandatory training for anyone liable to be exposed to asbestos fibres at work (see Regulation 10). This includes maintenance workers and others who may come into contact with or who may disturb asbestos (e.g. cable installers) as well as those involved in asbestos removal work.

When work with asbestos or which may disturb asbestos is being carried out, the **Control of Asbestos Regulations** require employers and the self-employed to prevent exposure to asbestos fibres. Where this is not reasonably practicable, they must make sure that exposure is kept as low as reasonably practicable by measures other than the use of respiratory protective equipment. The spread of asbestos must be prevented. The Regulations specify the work methods and controls that should be used to prevent exposure and spread.

Worker exposure must be below the airborne exposure limit (Control Limit). The **Control of Asbestos Regulations** have a single Control Limit for all types of asbestos of 0.1 fibres per cm^3 averaged over a four-hour reference period. A Control Limit is a maximum concentration of asbestos fibres in the air (averaged over any continuous four-hour period) that must not be exceeded.

In addition, short-term exposures must be strictly controlled and worker exposure should not exceed 0.6 fibres per cm^3 of air averaged over any continuous ten-minute period using respiratory protective equipment, if exposure cannot be reduced sufficiently using other means.

Respiratory protective equipment is an important part of the control regime but it must not be the sole measure used to reduce exposure and should only be used to supplement other measures. Work methods that control the release of fibres, such as those detailed in the HSE's *Asbestos Essentials* task sheets for non-licensed work, should be used. Respiratory protective equipment must be suitable, must fit properly and must ensure that worker exposure is reduced to as low as is reasonably practicable.

Most asbestos removal work must be undertaken by a licensed contractor but any decision on whether particular work is licensable is based on the risk. Work is only exempt from licensing if:

◆ the exposure of employees to asbestos fibres is sporadic and of low intensity (but exposure cannot be considered to be sporadic and of low intensity if the concentration of asbestos in the air is liable to exceed 0.6 fibres per cm3 measured over ten minutes); and

◆ it is clear from the risk assessment that the exposure of any employee to asbestos will not exceed the Control Limit; and

◆ the work involves:

▸ short, non-continuous maintenance activities. Work can only be considered as short, non-continuous maintenance activities if any one person carries out work with these materials for less than one hour in a seven-day period. The total time spent by all workers on the work should not exceed a total of two hours.

▸ removal of materials in which the asbestos fibres are firmly linked in a matrix. Such materials include: asbestos cement; textured decorative coatings and paints which contain asbestos; articles of bitumen, plastic, resin or rubber which contain asbestos where their thermal or acoustic properties are incidental to their main purpose (e.g. vinyl floor tiles, electric cables, roofing felt); and other insulation products which may be used at high temperatures but have no insulation purposes, e.g. gaskets, washers, ropes and seals.

▸ encapsulation or sealing of asbestos-containing materials which are in good condition, or

▸ air monitoring and control, and the collection and analysis of samples to find out if a specific material contains asbestos.

Under the **Control of Asbestos Regulations**, anyone carrying out work on asbestos insulation, asbestos coating or Asbestos Insulating Board (AIB) needs a licence issued by the HSE unless they meet one of the exemptions above.

If the work is licensable you have a number of additional duties. You need to:

◆ Notify the enforcing authority responsible for the site where you are working (e.g. HSE or the local authority).

◆ Designate the work area (see Regulation 18 for details).

◆ Prepare specific asbestos emergency procedures.

◆ Pay for your employees to undergo medical surveillance.

Within the criteria set out above for licensed asbestos work, it is still possible that non-licensed work could be carried out on materials that might release fibres when disturbed (friable) or deteriorate once worked on. Consequently, an additional category of work, **notifiable non-licensed work**, has been introduced in the **Control of Asbestos Regulations 2012** to ensure that this type of work, although non-licensed, should be notified to the enforcing authority. Therefore, non-licensed work is only non-notifiable if the work involves:

◆ Short, non-continuous maintenance activities **in which only non-friable materials are handled**.

◆ Removal **without deterioration of non-degraded** materials in which the asbestos fibres are firmly linked in a matrix.

So, to summarise, the three categories of work with asbestos are:

◆ Licensed work, which is subject to the full requirements of the **Control of Asbestos Regulations 2012.**

◆ Non-licensed work, which is exempt from the following:

  ▸ Notification.

  ▸ Medical examination.

  ▸ Health records.

  ▸ Arrangements to deal with incidents.

  ▸ Designation of asbestos areas.

◆ Notifiable non-licensed work, which is exempt from:

  ▸ Arrangements to deal with incidents.

  ▸ Designation of asbestos areas.

The **Control of Asbestos Regulations** require any analysis of the concentration of asbestos in the air to be measured in accordance with ISO 17025 which is the international standard for laboratory quality systems and the globally accepted basis for laboratory accreditation.

CONTROL OF LEAD AT WORK REGULATIONS 2002 AS AMENDED (SI 2002 NO. 2676)

These Regulations came into force on 21 November 2002 and replace earlier regulations. They require an employer to undertake a risk assessment (Reg. 5) in regard to his employees' exposure to lead and to prevent or control exposure to lead by putting measures in place, such as avoiding the use of lead, designing the process to minimise exposure, providing adequate ventilation systems or providing personal protective equipment where adequate control of exposure cannot be achieved by other means (Reg. 6), air monitoring (Reg. 9) and medical surveillance (Reg. 10).

◆ An occupational exposure limit for lead in air is set and must not be exceeded.

◆ Employees at risk must be monitored against a blood-lead suspension level. Blood-lead readings which exceed the action levels require the employer to investigate and remedy the cause.

◆ Women of child-bearing age and young people are subject to lower blood-lead suspension and action levels.

◆ Employees who are liable to be exposed to lead through work must be provided with suitable and sufficient information, instruction and training.

CONTROL OF MAJOR ACCIDENT HAZARDS REGULATIONS 2015 (COMAH) (SI 2015 NO. 483)

These Regulations came into force on 1 June 2015, replacing the 1999 Regulations of the same name.

Duties are placed on operators at either a lower tier level or upper tier formerly 'Top tier') level, these being defined by the quantity of dangerous substances used or stored. Thresholds are set individually for some of the more common substances, but otherwise thresholds apply for generic categories such as flammable gases. Operators are to notify the HSE before the inventories exceed the threshold quantities.

The Regulations place a general duty on operators to take all measures necessary to prevent major accidents and limit their consequences to people and the environment.

All lower tier and upper tier sites are obliged to have a Major Accident Prevention Policy (MAPP).

For upper tier sites, the main requirements are:

◆ Prepare a **safety report** demonstrating safe operation.

◆ Provide **information** to neighbours within a public information zone around the site defined by the HSE.

◆ Report **modifications** to installations to the HSE in advance of making them.

◆ Prepare and update **on-site (internal) emergency plans**.

◆ Provide information for the authorities to prepare **off-site (external) emergency plans**.

© RRC International

CONTROL OF NOISE AT WORK REGULATIONS 2005 (SI 2005 NO. 1643)

These Regulations identify exposure action and limit values. Where exposures to noise vary markedly from day to day, weekly personal noise exposures may be used instead of daily exposures. The values are as follows:

◆ **Lower Exposure Action Values**

  ▸ A daily or weekly personal noise exposure of 80 dB (A-weighted).

  ▸ A peak sound pressure of 135 dB (C-weighted).

  Where it is likely that a lower exposure action value may be exceeded, employers must carry out a risk assessment.

  At or above this level, employees must be provided with information about the likely noise exposure and the associated risk to hearing, the control measures in place to reduce exposure, hearing protection and health surveillance (hearing tests).

◆ **Upper Exposure Action Values**

  ▸ A daily or weekly personal noise exposure of 85 dB (A-weighted).

  ▸ A peak sound pressure of 137 dB (C-weighted).

  At or above this level, the employer must reduce exposure to as low a level as is reasonably practicable by establishing and implementing a programme of organisational and technical measures. The provision of hearing protectors is a last resort and is only acceptable when other methods of reducing exposure are not reasonably practicable.

  If the risk assessment indicates an employee is likely to be exposed to noise at or above an upper exposure action value, the employer shall ensure that the area is designated a Hearing Protection Zone, demarcated and identified by "Ear protection must be worn" signs, and that access to the area is restricted.

  Health surveillance (hearing checks) must be provided for all employees likely to be exposed regularly above the upper exposure action value.

◆ **Exposure Limit Values**

  ▸ A daily or weekly personal noise exposure of 87 dB (A-weighted).

  ▸ A peak sound pressure of 140 dB (C-weighted).

  These limits must not be exceeded. However, if an exposure limit value is exceeded, the employer must investigate the reason for the occurrence and identify and implement actions to ensure that it does not occur again.

The lower and upper exposure action values do not take account of any hearing protection. The exposure limit values do take account of hearing protection.

Risk Assessment

"In conducting the risk assessment, the employer shall assess the levels of noise to which workers are exposed by means of:

(a) *observation of specific working practices;*

(b) *reference to relevant information on the probable levels of noise corresponding to any equipment used in the particular working conditions; and*

(c) *if necessary, measurement of the level of noise to which his employees are likely to be exposed...." (Reg. 5).*

The risk assessment required by the Regulations should consider:

◆ The level, type and duration of exposure, including any exposure to peak sound pressure.

◆ The effects of exposure to noise on employees or groups of employees whose health is at particular risk from such exposure.

◆ Any effects on the health and safety of employees resulting from the interaction between noise and the use of ototoxic substances at work, or between noise and vibration.

◆ Any indirect effects on the health and safety of employees resulting from the interaction between noise and audible warning signals or other sounds that need to be audible in order to reduce risk at work.

◆ Any information provided by the manufacturers of work equipment.

◆ The availability of alternative equipment designed to reduce the emission of noise.

◆ Any extension of exposure to noise at the workplace beyond normal working hours, including exposure in rest facilities supervised by the employer.

◆ Appropriate information obtained following health surveillance, including, where possible, published information.

◆ The availability of personal hearing protectors with adequate attenuation characteristics.

Health Surveillance

If the risk assessment indicates that there is a risk to the health of his employees who are, or are liable to be, exposed to noise, the employer shall ensure that such employees are placed under suitable health surveillance, which shall include testing of their hearing.

CONTROL OF SUBSTANCES HAZARDOUS TO HEALTH REGULATIONS 2002 (COSHH) AS AMENDED (SI 2002 NO. 2677)

The **COSHH Regulations** were originally enacted in 1988, and have been frequently amended and re-enacted.

◆ A **substance** means a natural or artificial substance whether in solid or liquid form or in the form of a gas or vapour (including micro-organisms).

◆ A **substance hazardous to health** means:

  ▸ A substance, including a mixture:

    − Which is listed in Table 3.2 of Part 3 of Annex VI of the **CLP Regulation** and for which an indication of danger specified for the substance is very toxic, toxic, harmful, corrosive or irritant.

    − For which the Health and Safety Executive has approved a Workplace Exposure Limit (WEL).

    − Which is a biological agent.

    − Which is dust of any kind, except dust which is a substance within the above categories when present at specified concentrations in air.

  ▸ Any other substance creating a comparable hazard not listed above.

A Workplace Exposure Limit for a substance hazardous to health means the exposure limit approved by the HSE for the substance in relation to the specific reference period, when calculated by the approved method, as contained in EH40/2005 *Workplace Exposure Limits*.

There is a duty on an employer to undertake suitable and sufficient health risk assessment wherever an employee is liable to be exposed to a substance hazardous to health.

Other duties on employers include:

◆ Carrying out a **risk assessment** before carrying out work involving substances hazardous to health and where employees are liable to be exposed to these substances in the course of their work.

◆ **Reviewing** the **risk assessment** regularly or at such times where there is a **significant change to the work**.

◆ **Preventing or controlling** exposure to substances hazardous to health by applying a hierarchy of **measures** to control exposure and, as a last resort, providing suitable **PPE** and **RPE**.

◆ **Maintaining** exposures below any relevant workplace exposure limit or identifying reasons for exceeding it and taking appropriate action.

◆ **Monitoring** exposure at the workplace and installing measures in the event of failure of a **carcinogen** control measure.

◆ Ensuring control measures, PPE, etc. are **properly maintained, used** or **applied**.

◆ Ensuring employees, where appropriate, are under **health surveillance**.

◆ Providing **information, instruction and training** for employees who could be exposed.

◆ Implementing means for the **safe collection, storage** and **disposal** of contaminated biological waste and instituting safe working procedures and hygiene measures with the aim of preventing or reducing the accidental transfer or release of a biological agent from the workplace.

◆ Undertaking **fumigations** and issuing appropriate warning notices at all points of access to the premises or to the parts of premises where fumigations are to be carried out.

Duties on employees include:

◆ Making full and proper use of control measures, PPE, etc.

◆ Presenting themselves, where required, for health surveillance.

CONTROL OF VIBRATION AT WORK REGULATIONS 2005 (SI 2005 NO. 1093)

These Regulations apply to both hand-arm and whole-body vibration and make provision for action and limit values for daily exposure; the approach is very similar to that applied to noise. Limit values must not be exceeded, although there are provisions for weekly averaging in specified circumstances.

© RRC International

Under Regulation 4, values are specified for **hand-arm vibration**:

◆ The daily exposure limit value is 5 m/s^2 A(8).

◆ The daily exposure action value is 2.5 m/s^2 A(8).

The daily exposure is to be ascertained on the basis of Schedule 1, Part 1.

For **whole-body vibration**:

◆ The daily exposure limit value is 1.15 m/s^2 A(8).

◆ The daily exposure action value is 0.5 m/s^2 A(8).

The daily exposure is to be ascertained on the basis of Schedule 2, Part 1.

Under Regulation 5, the employer must carry out a **risk assessment** of those employees liable to be exposed to vibration risk and identify measures necessary to meet the requirements of the Regulations. The employer must assess the daily exposure to vibration by means of:

◆ Observation of specific working practices.

◆ Reference to relevant information on the probable magnitude of vibration corresponding to the equipment used in the particular working conditions.

◆ If necessary, measuring the magnitude of vibration to which his employees are liable to be exposed.

The risk assessment shall include consideration of:

◆ The magnitude, type and duration of exposure, including any intermittent vibration or repeated shocks.

◆ The effects of vibration exposure on employees at risk.

◆ Any effects of vibration on work equipment and the workplace, including handling of controls, indicator reading, structural stability and security of joints.

◆ Any information provided by work equipment manufacturers.

◆ Availability of replacement equipment which is designed to reduce vibration exposure.

◆ Any extension of whole-body vibration exposure beyond normal working hours and in employer-supervised rest facilities.

◆ Specific working conditions such as low temperatures.

◆ Appropriate health surveillance information, including published information.

The risk assessment must be reviewed regularly and if there has been a significant change in the work to which the assessment relates.

Regulation 6 requires the employer either to **eliminate the vibration exposure risk at source** or, where not reasonably practicable, **reduce to as low a level as is reasonably practicable**. Where it is not reasonably practicable to eliminate risk at source and an exposure action value is likely to be reached or exceeded, the employer shall reduce exposure to as low a level as is reasonably practicable by establishing and implementing a programme of organisational and technical measures which is appropriate to the activity. The measures to be taken by the employer are based on the general principles of prevention set out in the **Management of Health and Safety at Work Regulations 1999**, Schedule 1.

Regulation 7 requires the employer to place under appropriate **health surveillance** those employees whom the risk assessment indicates are at risk from, or liable to be exposed to, vibration; and those employees who are likely to be exposed to vibration at or above an exposure action value. He must keep health records. Where an employee is found to have an identifiable disease or adverse vibration health effect, the employer shall assign the employee to alternative work where there is no further risk of vibration exposure.

Information, **instruction** and **training** must be provided under Regulation 8.

CORPORATE LIABILITY

A corporate body can be held liable for most criminal offences provided that:

◆ it is a fineable offence;

◆ it is committed by a controlling mind, such as a director; and

◆ it is committed in the course of his or her corporate duties.

A corporate body can be held vicariously liable in cases where an ordinary master/ employer/agent would be held vicariously liable.

The method by which the corporation is held personally liable for the offences committed by the controlling mind is known as the *alter ego* doctrine.

Section 37 of the **Health and Safety at Work, etc. Act 1974** allows for individual directors to be prosecuted along with the company itself.

Functional directors, senior managers, company secretaries, other similar officers of a company, and any person purporting to act as any of the above may be individually liable under S.37 and/or for manslaughter at common law.

© RRC International

The statutory offence of corporate manslaughter (known as corporate homicide in Scotland) provides a way for action to be taken against companies when the responsibility cannot be attributed to an individual or individuals.

CORPORATE MANSLAUGHTER AND CORPORATE HOMICIDE ACT 2007

The **Corporate Manslaughter and Corporate Homicide Act 2007**, which came into force on 6 April 2008, introduced a new offence for prosecuting companies and other organisations where there has been a gross failing, throughout the organisation, in the management of health and safety with fatal consequences. Although it is not part of health and safety law, it introduced an important new element in the corporate management of health and safety.

The new offence is called corporate manslaughter in England, Wales and Northern Ireland, but corporate homicide in Scotland.

The common law offence of manslaughter by gross negligence is abolished in its application to corporations.

The Act also largely removes the Crown immunity that applied to the existing common law corporate manslaughter offence.

Companies and organisations can now be found guilty of corporate manslaughter as a result of serious management failures resulting in a gross breach of a duty of care. Prosecutions will be of the corporate body and not individuals, but the liability of directors, board members or other individuals under health and safety law or general criminal law will be unaffected, and both the corporate body itself and individuals can still be prosecuted for separate health and safety offences. However, an individual cannot be guilty of aiding, abetting, counselling or procuring the commission of an offence of corporate manslaughter/homicide.

An organisation will be guilty of an offence if the way in which its activities are managed or organised:

(a) causes a person's death, and

(b) amounts to a gross breach of a relevant duty of care owed by the organisation to the deceased, but only if the way in which its activities are managed or organised by its senior management is a substantial element in the breach (Sections 1 and 3).

A breach of a duty of care by an organisation is a "gross" breach if the conduct alleged to amount to a breach of that duty falls far below what can reasonably be expected of the organisation in the circumstances.

In relation to a 'gross breach' the jury must consider whether the evidence shows that the organisation failed to comply with any health and safety legislation that relates to the alleged breach, and if so:

(a) how serious that failure was;

(b) how much of a risk of death it posed (Section 8(2)).

The jury may also:

(a) consider the extent to which the evidence shows that there were attitudes, policies, systems or accepted practices within the organisation that were likely to have encouraged any such failure as is mentioned in Section 8(2), or to have produced tolerance of it;

(b) have regard to any health and safety guidance that relates to the alleged breach (Section 8(3)).

A "relevant duty of care", in relation to an organisation, means any of the following duties owed by it under the law of negligence:

(a) a duty owed to its employees or to other persons working for the organisation or performing services for it;

(b) a duty owed as occupier of premises;

(c) a duty owed in connection with:

- the supply by the organisation of goods or services (whether for consideration or not),
- the carrying on by the organisation of any construction or maintenance operations,
- the carrying on by the organisation of any other activity on a commercial basis, or
- the use or keeping by the organisation of any plant, vehicle or other thing;

(d) a duty owed to a person who is someone for whose safety the organisation is responsible, including somebody in custody (Section 2(1)).

"Senior management", in relation to an organisation, means the persons who play significant roles in:

◆ the making of decisions about how the whole or a substantial part of its activities are to be managed or organised, or

◆ the actual managing or organising of the whole or a substantial part of those activities (Section 1(4)(c)).

© RRC International

An organisation that is guilty of corporate manslaughter or corporate homicide is liable on conviction on indictment to a fine. However, the court may also make a "remedial order" requiring the organisation to take specified steps to remedy:

(a) the relevant breach;

(b) any matter that appears to the court to have resulted from the relevant breach and to have been a cause of the death;

(c) any deficiency, as regards health and safety matters, in the organisation's policies, systems or practices of which the relevant breach appears to the court to be an indication (Section 9(1)).

Furthermore, a court may make a "publicity order" requiring the organisation to publicise in a specified manner:

(a) the fact that it has been convicted of the offence;

(b) specified particulars of the offence;

(c) the amount of any fine imposed;

(d) the terms of any remedial order made (Section 10(1)).

COURT HIERARCHY (ENGLAND AND WALES)

There are two distinct systems - those courts dealing with **criminal matters** and those dealing with **civil matters**.

Criminal cases are heard initially in the Magistrates' Court and may be referred to the Crown Court.

◆ The **Magistrates' Court** is the lowest of the courts; magistrates hear cases and sentence for the less serious offences. They also hold preliminary examinations into indictable offences to ascertain whether the prosecution can show a *prima facie* case, as a result of which the accused may be committed for trial at the Crown Court.

◆ The **Crown Court** deals with serious criminal charges (indictable offences and 'hybrid' offences) and appeals from Magistrates' Courts.

The County Courts deal with civil matters only, e.g. civil claims in respect of negligence, breach of contract, etc.

The High Court of Justice deals with more important or more complex civil matters.

The three divisions of the High Court are Queen's Bench (contracts and torts), Chancery (land, wills, partnerships, companies, etc.) and Family.

The Queen's Bench division has supervisory functions over the lower courts and tribunals.

The Court of Appeal has two divisions: Civil Division, which hears appeals from County Courts and the High Court; and Criminal Division, which hears appeals from the Crown Courts.

The Supreme Court (a role formerly fulfilled by the appellate committee of the House of Lords) hears appeals on important legal matters from the Court of Appeal and, in some cases, from the High Court.

The European Court of Justice is the supreme law court as regards matters of EU law. It has no direct jurisdiction over purely domestic law, i.e. that law which is not founded on EU law and does not come into conflict with it. Its decisions on matters affecting EU law are enforceable through the network of courts and tribunals in all member states.

CRIMINAL COURT PROCEDURE

Procedures in the criminal courts take the following forms.

A defendant, one who is accused of a crime, can be brought before the court either by:

◆ a **summons**, namely a written order, signed by a magistrate, ordering that person to appear before a certain court on a certain date at a specified time to answer the accusation, which is the principal means; or

◆ a **warrant**, namely a written authority issued by a magistrate, addressed to a constable directing him to carry out some specified act, namely to arrest the person named in the warrant, and to bring that person before the court.

A summons is served by post or by hand, usually by a police constable.

An indictment is drawn up if the trial is to be dealt with in the Crown Court.

Proceedings for health and safety offences can be commenced only by an HSE Inspector or with the consent of the Director of Public Prosecutions.

Offences under the **Health and Safety at Work, etc. Act 1974** can be prosecuted as:

◆ triable only **summarily** - Magistrates' Court;

◆ triable **either way** - Magistrates' or Crown Court;

◆ triable only on **indictment** - Crown Court;

depending on the seriousness of the offence.

© RRC International

Prosecution procedure takes the following steps:

- **Information** is laid before the magistrate or clerk to the justice.

- The examining magistrate decides whether there is a charge to be answered.

- The magistrate decides whether the charge will be tried **summarily** or on **indictment**:

  - If tried **summarily**, the decision is explained to the defendant, who consents or otherwise to the summary trial.

  - A defendant charged with an **indictable only** offence now goes direct to the Crown Court.

The committal system is governed by S. 47 and Sch. 1 of the **Criminal Procedure and Investigations Act 1996**.

Bail may be granted to the accused pending trial, depending on the severity of the offence, and the accused can appeal to a judge in chambers where bail is refused.

Not all witnesses need attend a Magistrates' Court hearing, as a written statement may (or may not) be accepted as evidence.

Two sides are involved - the prosecution and the defence.

In Magistrates' Courts the procedure is governed by the **Magistrates' Courts Act 1980**, whereby the charge is read out and the defendant asked to state whether he/she is guilty or not guilty.

Where the defendant denies the charge, witnesses may be called and the evidence of witnesses challenged through the process of cross-examination.

After the cross-examination stage, the magistrates make a decision. On conviction, the defendant will be sentenced.

In the Crown Court, a jury decides on guilt or otherwise, and a judge decides on the sentence.

Crown Court procedure is as follows:

- Firstly, there is an **arraignment**, namely the calling of the defendant by name to answer the matter charged at the bar and to plead guilty, not guilty, or stand mute.

- Where a **not guilty** plea is entered, a jury will be sworn in. Procedure takes the form of reading the prosecution charge and the giving of evidence. Upon the closing of the prosecution case, the defence may make a submission of **no case to answer**.

◆ Where **no case to answer** is accepted by the judge, the jury is directed to find not guilty; where this submission is rejected, the trial continues, with the defendant and witnesses giving evidence. On completion of the evidence and cross-examination stage, the judge sums up and the jury considers the verdict.

◆ A judge may accept a **majority verdict** of not less than 10:2. Where a jury cannot agree a verdict, the judge may make a direction to return a **not guilty** verdict.

◆ On a **guilty** verdict, the judge can hear evidence of both good and bad character which he or she may or may not take into consideration. The judge may impose a sentence or discharge the accused; i.e. he or she may impose a fine and/or imprisonment, suspended sentence, conditional discharge, absolute discharge, etc.

CRIMINAL LIABILITY

This refers to the responsibilities of persons mainly under statutes and regulations (and also the common law, e.g. manslaughter) and the penalties that can be imposed by the criminal courts.

A crime or breach of criminal law is an offence against the State.

In health and safety legislation there are several levels of liability: **absolute, as far as practicable**, and **so far as is reasonably practicable**.

The burden of proving a criminal charge beyond reasonable doubt rests with the prosecution.

Where a person is found guilty, a court will impose some form of punishment, such as a fine or imprisonment or both.

Compensation may be ordered by a court to be paid to a person to cover personal injury and damage to property.

Cases are heard in the Magistrates' Courts and in the Crown Court.

The more serious cases are heard in the Crown Court before a judge and jury.

© RRC International

D

DAMAGES

Civil liability consists of an award of damages for injury, disease or death at work and/ or damage to property in circumstances disclosing a breach of common law (normally negligence) and/or statutory duty on the part of an employer/occupier of premises, arising out of and in the course of employment.

General damages relate to the pain, suffering and loss of amenity incurred as a result of the accident as well as to losses incurred after the hearing of the action, e.g. actual and probable loss of future earnings following an accident.

Special damages relate to quantifiable losses incurred before the hearing of the case, and consist mainly of medical expenses and loss of earnings from the date of the accident to the date of trial.

In the case of fatal injury, compensation for death negligently caused is payable under the **Fatal Accidents Act 1976**, and a fixed lump sum is payable under the **Administration of Justice Act 1982** in respect of bereavement.

DANGEROUS SUBSTANCES AND EXPLOSIVE ATMOSPHERES REGULATIONS 2002 (DSEAR) AS AMENDED (SI 2002 NO. 2776)

These Regulations impose requirements for the purpose of eliminating or reducing risks to safety from fire, explosion or other events arising from the hazardous properties of a dangerous substance in connection with work. A dangerous substance is:

(a) a substance or mixture which meets the criteria for classification as hazardous within any physical hazard class laid down in the **CLP Regulation**, whether or not the substance is classified under that Regulation;

(b) a substance or mixture which because of its physico-chemical or chemical properties and the way it is used or is present at the workplace creates a risk, not being a substance or mixture falling within subparagraph (a) above; or

(c) any dust, whether in the form of solid particles or fibrous materials or otherwise, which can form an explosive mixture with air or an explosive atmosphere, not being a substance or mixture falling within subparagraphs (a) or (b) above.

From June 2015, the Regulations also cover substances that are corrosive to metals and gases under pressure to allow for changes in the EU **Chemical Agents Directive**.

Regulation 3 contains disapplications in respect of certain provisions of the Regulations.

The duties under the Regulations on an employer in relation to his employees extend to non-employees, with certain savings. The duties also extend to self-employed persons.

Regulation 5 requires an employer to carry out a suitable and sufficient assessment of the risks to his employees where a dangerous substance is or may be present at the workplace.

Employers are required by Regulation 6 to eliminate or reduce risk so far as is reasonably practicable. Where risk is not eliminated, employers are required, so far as is reasonably practicable and consistent with the risk assessment, to apply measures to control risks and mitigate any detrimental effects.

Places at the workplace where explosive atmospheres may occur must be classified as hazardous or non-hazardous and hazardous places must be classified into zones on the basis of the frequency and duration of the occurrence of an explosive atmosphere (Regulation 7(1) and Schedule 2). Equipment and protective systems in hazardous places must comply with the requirements of Schedule 3 (Regulation 7(2)) and, where necessary, hazardous places must be marked with signs at their points of entry in accordance with Schedule 4 (Regulation 7(3)).

Employers are required under Regulation 8 to make arrangements for dealing with accidents, incidents and emergencies, and under Regulation 9 to provide employees with precautionary information, instruction and training where a dangerous substance is present at the workplace.

Containers and pipes used at work for dangerous substances must, where not already marked in accordance with the requirements of the legislation listed in Schedule 5, clearly identify their contents (Regulation 10).

Where two or more employers share a workplace where an explosive atmosphere may occur, the employer responsible for the workplace is to co-ordinate the implementation of the measures required by these Regulations (Regulation 11).

DANGEROUS SUBSTANCES (NOTIFICATION AND MARKING OF SITES) REGULATIONS 1990 AS AMENDED (SI 1990 NO. 304)

These Regulations are principally directed at the safety of fire authority personnel attending incidents at premises containing large quantities of dangerous substances. The Regulations apply where the aggregate quantity of dangerous substances on a site is 25 tonnes or more.

© RRC International

Dangerous substances are those which are defined as dangerous for carriage under the Carriage of Dangerous Goods and Use of Transportable Pressure Equipment Regulations 2009.

The person in control of a site must notify both the HSE or the local authority, and the fire authority, prior to storage in excess of the aggregate quantity on site and mark the site accordingly.

All sites to which the Regulations apply (with the exception of petrol filling stations) must display the appropriate signs, namely access signs and location signs, which must be kept clean and free from obstruction.

DEFENCES (COMMON LAW)

There are several defences available to an employer sued for a breach of duties at common law:

◆ **No duty** was owed by the employer to the claimant. If the claimant is an employee who sustained injury while in the course of his or her employment, this defence is unlikely to succeed.

◆ The **duty** of care was **not breached**. Often the key battleground in a negligence claim, the defendant employer will attempt to demonstrate that they met the standard of care required of them and that everything reasonable had been done to protect others from injury, damage or other loss. If the court agrees, this will be a complete defence.

◆ The **breach did not lead to the loss**. It may be possible to show that, despite there being a breach in the duty of care, that breach was not a causative factor in the employee's loss or injury.

◆ The **nature of the injury** was **unforeseeable**. Employers cannot be expected to protect others against those things that a reasonably competent employer could not foresee.

◆ **Voluntary assumption of risk (***volenti non fit injuria***)** is a complete defence and means that no damages will be payable.

A *volenti* defence applies to a situation where an employee, being fully aware of the risks that he or she is taking in not complying with safety instructions, duties, etc. after being exhorted and supervised, and having received training and instruction in the risks involved in not following these instructions, procedures, etc., suffers injury, disease or death as a result of not complying with them. However, such a defence is unlikely to be successful nowadays, given the extent of health and safety legislation and common law case precedent.

◆ **Contributory negligence** can arise in situations where a claimant is partly to blame for his/her injury, death or disease.

Section 1 of the **Law Reform (Contributory Negligence) Act 1945** states that where a person suffers damage as the result partly of his own fault and partly of the fault of another person, a claim in respect of that damage shall not be defeated by reason of the fault of the person suffering the damage, but the damages recoverable in respect thereof shall be reduced to such extent as the court thinks just and equitable having regard to the claimant's share in the responsibility for the damage.

The claimant may, however, plead *res ipsa loquitur* (the thing speaks for itself), a term that commonly arises in civil actions, implying that the defendant was negligent or careless, or that if he had taken proper precautions or ordered his work correctly, the damage would not have arisen, i.e. the negligence is self-evident.

DELEGATED (SUBORDINATE) LEGISLATION

This may take a number of forms:

◆ **Orders in Council** - not commonly used except in times of national emergency. They are used to give the force of law to administrative regulations drawn up by a government department.

◆ **Statutory Instruments** - the most common form of delegated legislation, made by the Minister responsible for the implementation of a statute and taking the form of regulations. Power to make regulations is incorporated in the statute; statutory instruments made under the **Health and Safety at Work, etc. Act 1974** include the **Control of Substances Hazardous to Health Regulations 2002, as amended**, and the **Safety Representatives and Safety Committees Regulations 1977, as amended**.

◆ **By-Laws** - local authorities and statutory undertakings have the power to make by-laws to regulate a whole range of issues. Power to make by-laws is given in the statute and examples include by-laws for street markets, control of animals, loud amplification equipment, etc.

DESIGNERS', MANUFACTURERS', ETC. DUTIES (HSWA)

The duties of designers, manufacturers, etc., are stated in a wide range of legislation, which includes the **Construction (Design and Management) Regulations 2015**; **Consumer Protection Act 1987**; **Carriage of Dangerous Goods and Use of Transportable Pressure Equipment Regulations 2009**; **Control of Noise at Work Regulations 2005**;

© RRC International

Provision and Use of Work Equipment Regulations 1998; European Communities Act 1972 and the Supply of Machinery (Safety) Regulations 2008.

The requirements of Section 6 of the Health and Safety at Work, etc. Act 1974 include:

◆ Ensuring the design and construction are safe and without risks to health.

◆ Testing and examination.

◆ Providing adequate information.

◆ Conducting research to eliminate or minimise risks.

◆ Ensuring erectors/installers do their jobs correctly.

The above provisions generally apply to articles and substances in use at work and also to fairground equipment.

DISCLOSURE OF INFORMATION

Section 28 of the Health and Safety at Work, etc. Act 1974 requires that no person shall disclose any information obtained by him as a result of the exercise of any power conferred by Sections 14 or 20 (including, in particular, any information with respect to any trade secret obtained by him in any premises entered by him by virtue of any such power) except:

◆ for the purposes of his **functions**; or

◆ for the purposes of any **legal proceedings, investigation or inquiry,** or for the purposes of a **report** of any such proceedings or inquiry or of a **special report** made by virtue of Section 14; or

◆ with the **relevant consent**.

Information must not normally be disclosed except with the consent of the person providing it.

Disclosure may be made in certain cases:

◆ for the purposes of any **legal proceedings, investigation or inquiry** held at the request of the HSE;

◆ with the relevant consent;

◆ for providing **employees or their representatives** with health-and-safety-related information.

See also **Public Interest Disclosure Act 1998** (noted under **EMPLOYMENT RIGHTS ACT 1996** below).

DOUBLE-BARRELLED ACTION

In principle, an employee is entitled to sue his or her employer for damages for injury resulting from a breach of a duty at common law (i.e. negligence) and a breach of statutory duty in certain situations (the double-barrelled action).

An injured employee sues separately, though simultaneously, for a breach of both duties by the employer.

This form of action can be traced back to *Kilgollan v. Cooke & Co. Ltd (1956)*, a case which involved the fencing provisions of the **Factories Act 1937**. (Note: Guarding provisions are now in the **Provision and Use of Work Equipment Regulations 1998**.)

However (see **CIVIL LIABILITY - BREACH OF STATUTORY DUTY**), Section 69 of the **Enterprise and Regulatory Reform Act 2013** significantly changes a claimant's approach to civil actions against an employer for health and safety breaches and amends Section 47 of the **Health and Safety at Work, etc. Act 1974** to require that there should be no civil right of action for breach of a duty imposed by certain health and safety legislation, other than where such a right is specifically provided for. Claimants will now need to show that an employer has been negligent under the common law rules of tort and employers will no longer be strictly liable for civil claims for breach of health and safety duties.

An exception to this arises from amendments to the **Management of Health and Safety at Work Regulations 1999** which allow new mothers and pregnant workers to bring a civil claim for breach of those Regulations which impose specific duties on employers in relation to such employees.

DUE DILIGENCE DEFENCE

A statutory defence of due diligence is available under certain statutes and regulations, e.g.:

◆ **Control of Substances Hazardous to Health Regulations 2002**, Reg. 21.

◆ **Food Safety Act 1990**, S.21.

◆ **Confined Spaces Regulations 1997**, Reg. 7.

◆ **Electricity at Work Regulations 1989**, S.29.

This defence is not available under the **Health and Safety at Work, etc. Act 1974**.

Some statutes/regulations state, "It shall be a defence for any person to prove that he took all reasonable precautions and exercised all due diligence to avoid the commission of that offence," or "It shall be a defence for the person charged to prove that he took all reasonable precautions and exercised all due diligence to avoid the commission of the offence by himself or by a person under his control."

© RRC International

DUTY OF CARE

At common law, employers must take reasonable care to protect their employees from the risks of foreseeable injury, disease or death at work and/or damage to their property. This liability is based on *Donoghue v. Stevenson (1932)*.

If an employer is aware of a health and safety risk to employees or ought, in the light of current knowledge at that time, to have known of the existence of a hazard, he will be liable if an employee is injured or killed or suffers illness as a result of the risk, or if the employer failed to take reasonable care to avoid this happening.

The common law duties of an employer were identified in general terms in *Wilsons & Clyde Coal Co. Ltd v. English (1938)*.

The common law requires that all employers provide and maintain:

◆ A safe place of work with safe means of access to and egress from it.

◆ Adequate training and supervision.

◆ Safe appliances, equipment and plant for doing the work.

◆ A safe system for doing that work.

◆ Competent and safety-conscious personnel.

These duties apply even though an employee may be working on a third party's premises or where an employee has been hired out to another employer, but where the control of the task still lies with the permanent employer.

The tests of whether or not an employee has been temporarily employed by another employer are:

◆ The **control test**.

◆ The **organisation test**.

◆ The **multiple test**.

Manufacturers and others can also be sued for negligence.

E

ELECTRICITY AT WORK REGULATIONS 1989 (SI 1989 NO. 635)

These Regulations apply to all work associated with electricity, and state general principles rather than detailed requirements. They impose duties on duty holders - employers, employees, and managers of mines and quarries.

Electrical equipment is defined as including anything used or installed for use to generate, provide, transmit, transform, rectify, convert, conduct, distribute, control, store, measure or use electrical energy.

The general requirements include the following:

◆ All **systems** to be constructed and maintained so as to prevent danger (risk of injury).

◆ **Work activities** to be carried out in such a manner as to prevent danger.

◆ **Protective equipment** to be suitable for its purpose, suitably maintained and properly used.

◆ No equipment to be put into use where its **strength and capability** may be exceeded in such a way as to give rise to danger.

◆ Equipment not to be exposed to **adverse or hazardous environments**.

◆ **Conductors** to be insulated or safe by position.

◆ Provision of **earthing** or other suitable precautions where a system may become electrically charged.

◆ Suitable precautions to be taken to maintain **integrity of referenced conductors**.

◆ **Joints and connections** to be mechanically and electrically suitable.

◆ Efficient means to be provided for protection against **excess current**.

◆ Suitable means to be provided for **cutting off** supply of electrical energy and the **isolation** of any circuit.

◆ Adequate precautions to be taken on **equipment made dead**.

◆ Adequate precautions to be taken on **work on or near live conductors**; live work is only permitted where it is unreasonable for the equipment to be dead.

© RRC International

◆ Adequate **working space**, **means of access and lighting** to be provided where necessary.

◆ **Competent persons** to be appointed where technical knowledge or experience is necessary to prevent danger.

A defence of all reasonable precautions and all due diligence is available.

EMPLOYEES' DUTIES (HSWA AND MHSWR)

◆ **Employees' duties under Sections 7 and 8 of the** Health and Safety at Work, etc. Act 1974 are:

  ▸ To take reasonable care for their own and others' safety.

  ▸ To co-operate with employers to ensure compliance.

  ▸ Not intentionally or recklessly to interfere with or misuse things provided in the interests of health, safety and welfare. (Note: This applies to persons generally, not just employees.)

◆ **An employee's duties under the** Management of Health and Safety at Work Regulations 1999 are:

  ▸ To use any machinery, equipment, dangerous substance, transport equipment, means of production or safety device in accordance with training, prohibitions and instructions given to him by the employer in pursuance of statutory duties.

  ▸ To inform the employer or supervisor, etc. of any work situation which represents a serious and immediate danger to health and safety and any shortcomings in the employer's protection measures which affect him.

Many other Regulations also lay down duties on employees.

EMPLOYERS' DUTIES (HSWA)

There is a general duty under Sections 2 and 3 of the **Health and Safety at Work, etc. Act 1974** to ensure the health, safety and welfare of all employees at work.

Specific duties include:

◆ The provision and maintenance of **plant** and **systems of work** that are safe and without risks to health **(S.2(2)(a))**.

◆ Making arrangements for ensuring safety and absence of risks to health in connection with the use, handling, storage and transport of **articles and substances (S.2(2)(b))**.

◆ The provision of **information, instruction, training and supervision** to ensure health and safety **(S.2(2)(c))**.

◆ The maintenance of a **safe workplace**, with safe **access** to and **egress** from it **(S.2(2)(d))**.

◆ The provision and maintenance of a safe **working environment** and adequate arrangements for **welfare** at work **(S.2(2)(e))**.

Employers have a duty to prepare and revise as necessary a Statement of Health and Safety Policy and to consult with safety representatives (S.2(3) and (4)). They have a duty not to charge employees in respect of anything done or provided to ensure legal compliance (S.9).

Duties of employers towards people other than their own employees (S.3) include the following:

◆ Non-employees not to be exposed to risks so far as is reasonably practicable.

◆ Non-employees to be provided with prescribed information that might affect their health and safety.

EMPLOYERS' LIABILITY

Under the **Employer's Liability (Defective Equipment) Act 1969** employers are strictly liable for injuries to employees caused by defective equipment.

An injury suffered by an employee is to be attributable to negligence by the employer:

◆ where an employee suffers personal injury (including death) in the course of employment in consequence of a defect in equipment;

◆ where the equipment was provided by the employer for use in his business; and

◆ where the defect is attributable, wholly or in part, to the fault of a third party, whether identified or not, such as a manufacturer, supplier, distributor or importer.

EMPLOYMENT MEDICAL ADVISORY SERVICE (EMAS)

This service was created by the **Employment Medical Advisory Service Act 1972** (now largely repealed) but now falls under Part II of the **Health and Safety at Work, etc. Act 1974**. EMAS advises the Secretary of State, the HSE, employers, employees, trainers and others concerned with the health and safety of employed persons on health-related issues at work.

© RRC International

The service provides medical assistance, appoints registered medical practitioners as Employment Medical Advisers (EMAs), and is responsible for the payment of fees to medical advisers, for the remuneration of persons attending examinations, and the keeping of records and accounts.

No information about a person may be disclosed to anyone other than for the efficient performance of the adviser's functions; an employee may, by consent, waive this restriction.

EMPLOYMENT RIGHTS ACT 1996 (ERA) AS AMENDED

ERA includes provisions giving employees the right to refer certain matters (e.g. unfair dismissal) to an employment tribunal and lays down minimum rights concerning:

◆ Statement of main terms of contract.

◆ Notice.

◆ Unfair dismissal.

◆ Redundancy.

◆ Guaranteed pay.

◆ Medical suspension pay.

◆ Maternity leave.

◆ Cashless pay.

◆ Time off for public duties/trade union activities, etc.

Subsequent legislation and amendments to the Act cover discrimination, equal pay/value, trade union collective rights, national minimum wage, working time, social security and transfer of undertakings. The **Employee Relations Act 1999** covers a number of areas such as:

◆ Family leave including improved maternity rights.

◆ Better compensation in employment tribunals.

◆ Better part-time workers' rights, etc.

The **Employment Act 2002** aims to build constructive employment relations and avoid the need for litigation through better communication in the workplace and improved conciliation. The Act encourages internal resolution of workplace disputes and places a requirement on employees to raise grievances with employers before applying to a tribunal. The Act also places a duty on employers to consider fairness and adaptability in terms of flexible working hours and conditions.

The **Public Interest Disclosure Act 1998** protects employees who "whistle blow" or give information in the public interest (e.g. exposure of poor health and safety practices) without risk of discipline, dismissal, etc. Workers must act in good faith and not for financial gain.

EMPLOYMENT TRIBUNALS

Employment tribunals deal with a wide range of statutory employment matters, including industrial relations issues, unfair dismissal, equal pay and sex discrimination, safety representatives' time off and pay, appeals against improvement and prohibition notices, national minimum wage, working time, etc.

They consist of a legally qualified chairperson, appointed by the Lord Chancellor, and two lay members, one from employers /the CBI and one from trade unions/the TUC. When all three members of a tribunal are sitting, the majority view prevails. The chairperson can sit alone in some cases.

Employment tribunals deal with the following employment/health and safety issues:

◆ Appeals against Improvement and Prohibition Notices.

◆ Time off for the training of Safety Representatives.

◆ Failure of an employer to pay a Safety Representative for time off undertaking his/her functions and training.

◆ Failure of an employer to make a medical suspension payment.

◆ Dismissal, actual or constructive, following a breach of health and safety law and/or a term of an employment contract.

◆ Dismissal for asserting health and safety rights automatically deemed unfair, especially if the employee believed himself to be in serious and imminent danger.

◆ Circumstances as listed in the **Employment Rights Act 1996**.

Industrial tribunals were renamed employment tribunals by the **Employment Rights (Dispute Resolution) Act 1998**. Procedures are governed by the **Employment Tribunals Act 1996**.

ENFORCEMENT

Enforcement of health and safety legislation is undertaken by Inspectors appointed under Section 19 of the **Health and Safety at Work, etc. Act 1974** and authorised by written warrant from the enforcing authority.

© RRC International

Enforcing Agencies

Enforcing agencies are:

◆ **Health and Safety Executive (HSE)** - factories, agricultural, offshore, etc. inspectorates.

◆ **Local authorities** - principally through their **environmental health departments** - service industries, shops, offices, etc.

◆ **Office of Rail Regulation** - railways.

◆ **Office for Nuclear Regulation** - nuclear installations.

◆ **Fire authorities** - for fire precautions in most premises under the **Regulatory Reform (Fire Safety) Order 2005**.

◆ **Environment Agency** - pollution control under environmental protection legislation.

It is worth noting that enforcement responsibilities can be (and have been) transferred between enforcement agencies. So, the above list is intended to be indicative rather than absolute.

Powers

HSE/EH Inspectors have the following powers:

◆ To **enter premises** at any reasonable time accompanied, if necessary, by police officers.

◆ To take with them any **duly authorised person**, **equipment or materials** required.

◆ To make **examinations and investigations**.

◆ To direct that any premises, any part thereof or anything therein shall **remain undisturbed** for the purposes of examination and investigation.

◆ To take **measurements, photographs, recordings and samples**.

◆ To cause any article or substance to be **dismantled or subjected to any process or test**.

◆ To **take possession** of any article or substance and **detain** for as long as is necessary.

◆ To require any person to **give information, answer questions and sign a declaration of truth**.

◆ To require production of, inspect and take copies of **books and documents** required to be maintained or otherwise.

- To require any person to afford **appropriate facilities and assistance**.
- To inform **Safety Representatives** of matters they have found following **an investigation or examination**.
- To serve **Improvement Notices** and **Prohibition Notices.**
- To **prosecute** offenders.

Improvement Notices

Improvement Notices are served on employers and other persons by enforcement officers when, in their opinion, a business is not complying with the law and action is required by a certain date.

The business can request a **written explanation** of the alleged breaches, an **outline** of remedial measures and a **date** for implementing measures, **before** the notice is issued.

The business has **two weeks** to make **representations** if it thinks the notice should be changed or not issued; if no representations are received, the notice is issued.

There is a **right of appeal** to an employment tribunal **against** the notice which suspends its enforcement until a decision is reached by the tribunal.

Prohibition Notices

Prohibition Notices are served by enforcement officers when they are of the opinion that a work activity involves or will involve a risk of serious personal injury. The notice places a prohibition on certain activities until remedial measures are implemented. It is not necessary for a legal provision to have been contravened, but that there is an immediate threat to life. A Prohibition Notice may be served with immediate effect or suspended. Appeal to a tribunal does not suspend the implementation of the requirements outlined in the notice.

EUROPEAN DIRECTIVES

Directives usually provide for harmonisation of the laws of the EU member states, including those covering occupational health and safety. Directives impose a duty on each member state to make legislation to conform to the Directive and to enforce such legislation.

Directives are legally binding on all governments as to the result to be achieved. This means that, although member states must implement the requirements of a directive, they can do so in whatever form they wish (in the UK this will normally be a Regulation) and include whatever content they wish provided the objectives of the directive are met and the implementing legislation does not adversely affect the growth and development of small and medium-sized enterprises.

© RRC International

Framework directives set out overall objectives which are subsequently dealt with individually in Daughter directives.

EUROPEAN UNION

The EU is administered by four bodies:

◆ **The Commission** - performs a civil-service-like function. It is headed by a body of Commissioners from member states and is sometimes referred to as "The Guardian of the treaties". The Commission is empowered to take action against any member state not complying with EU legislation. It can make proposals for future legislation to the Council of the European Union (formerly the Council of Ministers).

◆ **The Council of the European Union** - the final decision-making body in the EU. Governments of member states are represented on this body.

◆ **The European Parliament** - consists of members (MEPs) who represent constituencies in their own member states. The principal role of the European Parliament is to discuss EU proposals and it must be consulted on all proposed legislation.

◆ **The Court of Justice of the European Communities** (known as the 'European Court of Justice') - the supreme law court. Cases can only be brought before this court by organisations or individuals representing organisations.

F

FATAL ACCIDENTS AT WORK

Under the **Fatal Accidents Act 1976**, dependants of a person killed at work may claim compensation for financial loss suffered by them as a result of the death.

Where death is caused by any wrongful act, neglect or default which is such as would (if death had not ensued) have entitled the person injured to maintain an action and recover damages, the person who would have been liable if death had not ensued shall be liable for damages (S.1, **Fatal Accidents Act 1976**).

A lump sum is also payable to dependants (S.1A, **Fatal Accidents Act 1976**).

Subsequent remarriage or the prospect of remarriage of a dependant must not be taken into account in assessing fatal damages.

FIRE AUTHORITIES

Fire authorities have a duty to:

◆ Provide **services** for their area of a **fire brigade** and **equipment**.

◆ Provide **training** for members of the fire brigade.

◆ Make arrangements for dealing with **calls** and for **summoning** members of the fire brigade.

◆ Make arrangements for obtaining **information** required for fire-fighting purposes with regard to the character of buildings, the available water supplies, means of access and other material local circumstances.

◆ Make arrangements for ensuring that reasonable steps are taken to prevent or mitigate **damage** to property resulting from measures taken in dealing with fires.

◆ Make arrangements for the giving of **advice** in respect of buildings, etc., restricting the spread of fire and means of escape.

◆ Take all reasonable measures for ensuring provision of an **adequate water supply** for use in the event of fire.

Powers of the fire authority include the power to:

◆ Provide **accommodation** for the brigade and its equipment.

◆ **Pay** casual members of the brigade.

© RRC International

◆ Provide and maintain **fire alarms** in public places, including the **fixing** of such alarms.

◆ Operate **outside** their area where requested.

◆ Employ the brigade for purposes **other than fire-fighting** where suitable.

◆ **Secure** the use, in case of fire, of water under the control of another person other than statutory water undertakers, and improve **access** to any such water by carrying out maintenance in connection with the use of such water in case of fire.

FIRE SAFETY AND SAFETY OF PLACES OF SPORT ACT 1987 AS AMENDED

Part I of this Act, which dealt with fire certificates, means of escape and fire fighting, interim duties as to safety of premises, premises involving serious risks to persons, inspection of premises, civil and other liability, and further miscellaneous provisions was repealed by the **Regulatory Reform (Fire Safety) Order 2005** and the **Fire (Scotland) Act 2005 (Consequential Modifications and Savings) Order 2006.**

Part II remains in force and deals with issues such as spectator capacity, safety certificates, grounds involving serous risk to spectators, and enforcement.

Part III deals with the safety of stands at sports grounds.

Specific provisions for places of sport are as follows:

◆ A **general safety certificate** is required for any sports ground.

◆ The **Safety of Sports Grounds Act 1975** is extended to any sports ground that the Secretary of State considers appropriate.

◆ The validity of a safety certificate no longer requires the provision of a **police presence**, unless consent is given by a chief constable or chief police officer.

◆ There is provision for the service of **Prohibition Notices** in the case of serious risk to spectators, prohibiting or restricting the admission of spectators in general or on specified occasions.

◆ Sports grounds must be **inspected** at least once a year.

◆ A safety certificate is required for each **regulated stand**, i.e. one providing covered accommodation for 500 or more spectators.

FIRST AID

Regulation of first-aid facilities, training and duties of employers are covered by the **Health and Safety (First-Aid) Regulations 1981, as amended** (see separate entry).

G

GAS APPLIANCES

The current legislation controlling the installation and use of gas is the **Gas Safety (Installation and Use) Regulations 1998** which came into force in October 1998 and place duties on installers, landlords and some gas suppliers:

◆ All businesses which carry out work on gas appliances must be **registered** from 1 April 2009 with the Gas Safe Register operated by Capita. (Formerly the requirement was for registration with CORGI (Council for Registered Gas Installers).)

◆ Only a **competent person** may undertake work on gas appliances.

◆ A gas appliance which is known to be or suspected of being **faulty** must not be used.

◆ Registered installers have instructions from the HSE (through Capita) to **disconnect** any gas appliance which is so dangerous as to be a threat to life if used.

◆ **Landlords** are responsible for ensuring appliances are **maintained** in good order and **checked** for safety at least **every 12 months**; they must keep a **record** of safety checks and **show** them to the tenant if requested.

◆ There are **restrictions** on the installation in **sleeping accommodation** of gas appliances which are not of the **balanced flue type**:

  ▸ Non-balanced flue appliances of **less than 14 kilowatts** may be fitted as long as they have a **device which automatically turns off the gas supply** before a dangerous level of toxic fumes builds up.

  ▸ Non-balanced flue appliances above this threshold are prohibited in such accommodation.

The **Gas Appliances (Safety) Regulations 1995** apply to all appliances after January 1996, in that:

◆ Gas appliances and fittings must be safe when properly used and not present danger to persons, domestic animals or property.

◆ They must feature **comprehensive instructions** when sold both for the installer and the user.

◆ They must be accompanied by relevant **warning notices** regarding ventilation at the point of installation.

© RRC International

◆ **Design and construction** must be certified safe.

◆ All appliances and fittings must have an **EU mark** and a **certificate of approval**.

GLOBALLY HARMONISED SYSTEM (GHS)

The internationally agreed Globally Harmonised System of Classification and Labelling of Chemicals (GHS) has been implemented in the European Union by the Classification, Labelling and Packaging Regulation (CLP) (see earlier) under which there are:

◆ New **criteria** to assess hazardous properties of chemicals.

◆ New harmonised **hazard warning symbols** for labels (known as 'pictograms').

◆ New harmonised **hazard and precautionary statements** for labels, which replace the previous risk and safety phrases.

GOODS AND OTHER VEHICLES

Safety of goods and other vehicles should take into account the following:

◆ Properly adjusted and maintained **brakes and lights** must be provided on vehicles **used on public roads**, together with an **audible warning system**.

◆ **Loads** must be secure and safe by position.

◆ Every motor vehicle must be equipped with an appropriate **rear view mirror**.

◆ Vehicles must be fitted with an **exhaust silencer** and **speedometer**.

◆ **Any rope or chain** used for the purposes of **towing** must not exceed 4.5m in length.

◆ **Tyres** must be in good condition, with a specified **minimum depth of tread**.

◆ Goods vehicles must have **safety glass** fitted to the windscreen and side windows.

◆ The **Provision and Use of Work Equipment Regulations 1998** and the **Construction (Design and Management) Regulations 2015** apply on-site; off-site the **Road Traffic Acts** apply.

Specific provisions relating to drivers are:

◆ A good general state of health and good **eyesight**.

◆ Adherence to the **stipulated number of hours** spent driving and the **recording** of such hours.

◆ Refraining from **drinking alcohol**.

◆ Adherence to **speed limits**.

◆ Holding a current **driving licence** and **insurance**.

H

HEALTH AND SAFETY AT WORK, ETC. ACT 1974 (HSWA)

HSWA is an umbrella Act of general duties over, in some cases, former legislation such as the **Factories Act 1961** and the **Offices, Shops and Railway Premises Act 1963**.

HSWA Part I and former Acts specified in Schedule 1 of **HSWA** and any Regulations made under them are deemed to be the relevant statutory provisions with regard to **HSWA** by S.53(1).

Section 15 of **HSWA** gives the Secretary of State power to make Regulations which are part of the relevant statutory provisions. The relevant statutory provisions include:

◆ Part I of **HSWA**.

◆ Regulations made under Part I.

◆ The Acts contained in Schedule 1 of **HSWA**.

◆ Any Regulations made under the above Acts.

HSWA covers all people at work except domestic workers in private employment and extends to the prevention of risks to the health and safety of the general public.

The general objectives of **HSWA** are:

◆ To secure the health, safety and welfare of all persons at work.

◆ To protect others from the risks arising from workplace activities.

◆ To control the obtaining, keeping and use of explosive or highly flammable substances.

◆ To control emissions into the atmosphere of noxious or offensive substances (now largely contained in environmental protection legislation).

Some duties are qualified by "so far as is reasonably practicable" (see **ABSOLUTE AND QUALIFIED DUTIES**).

The police are now covered by **HSWA** by virtue of the **Police (Health and Safety) Act 1997**.

All employees and some others (with some exceptions) are covered by **HSWA** and Regulations made under the Act, including:

◆ The offshore oil and gas industry.

◆ Trainees.

◆ The self-employed.

© RRC International

Crown servants are covered but the HSE/Environmental Health Officers cannot enforce the law in Crown establishments. The forces can get exemption certificates under some Regulations.

HEALTH AND SAFETY AT WORK, ETC. ACT 1974 (GENERAL DUTIES OF SELF-EMPLOYED PERSONS) (PRESCRIBED UNDERTAKINGS) REGULATIONS 2015 (SI 2015 NO. 1583)

These Regulations specify the circumstances in which self-employed persons are required to comply with their duty under the **Health and Safety at Work, etc. Act 1974** to conduct their undertakings in such a way as to ensure, so far as reasonably practicable, that they themselves and other persons (not being their employees) who may be affected by their work activities are not exposed to risks to their health and safety.

Work activities covered include:

◆ Agriculture (including forestry).

◆ Any work with asbestos.

◆ Any work on a construction site.

◆ Any activity to which the **Gas Safety (Installation and Use) Regulations 1998** apply.

◆ Contained use within the meaning of Regulation 2(1) of the **Genetically Modified Organisms (Contained Use) Regulations 2014**.

◆ The operation of a railway.

◆ Any other activity that may pose a risk to the health and safety of another person (other than the self-employed person carrying it out or their employees).

HEALTH AND SAFETY (CONSULTATION WITH EMPLOYEES) REGULATIONS 1996 (SI 1996 NO. 1513)

These Regulations implement an EU Framework Directive which requires member states to introduce measures to encourage improvement in the health and safety of employees.

They apply in cases where employees are not already represented by trade-union-appointed Safety Representatives under the **Safety Representatives and Safety Committees Regulations 1977**.

The employer is required to consult with employees on health and safety matters, either directly or with elected employee representatives.

Employers must provide information to employees and/or their representatives and also training, time off and facilities to employee representatives, and establish suitable procedures, so as to enable them to participate effectively in consultations.

It is the employer's duty to consult with Safety Representatives, specified as follows:

◆ Concerning the introduction of any measure which may **substantially** affect the health and safety of employees that the representative represents.

◆ About arrangements for nominating **competent persons**.

◆ In relation to **information** he is required to provide under the relevant statutory provisions.

◆ On the planning and organisation of any **health and safety training**.

◆ With regard to the consequences of the introduction of **new technology**.

The employer is to provide facilities and assistance to enable Safety Representatives to carry out their functions (Reg. 17 which inserts Reg. 4A(1) into the **Safety Representatives and Safety Committees Regulations 1977**).

HEALTH AND SAFETY (DISPLAY SCREEN EQUIPMENT) REGULATIONS 1992 AS AMENDED (SI 1992 NO. 2792)

Display Screen Equipment (DSE) means any alphanumeric or graphic display screen, regardless of the display process involved. This includes flat panel screens, touch screens and other emerging technologies.

These Regulations apply to all defined users and operators:

◆ **User** means any **employee** who habitually uses DSE as a significant part of their normal work.

◆ **Operator** means any **self-employed person** who habitually uses DSE as a significant part of their normal work.

◆ **Workstation** means an assembly comprising the DSE, optional accessories, disk drive, telephone, modem, printer, etc., and the immediate work environment.

The Regulations do not apply to drivers' cabs or control cabs for vehicles or machinery, DSE on board a means of transport or mainly intended for public use, portable systems not in prolonged use, calculators, cash registers, etc., or window typewriters (but Regulation 3 of the **Management of Health and Safety at Work Regulations 1999** does apply).

There is a duty on employers to perform a suitable and sufficient analysis of workstations provided for users and operators.

© RRC International

Other duties on employers include:

◆ To ensure compliance with the Schedule to the Regulations.

◆ To plan the activities of users to ensure periodic **screen breaks or changes of activity**.

◆ To ensure that appropriate **eye and eyesight tests** are provided for users or when an employee becomes a defined user, at regular intervals thereafter and when a user experiences visual difficulties.

◆ To ensure provision of **special corrective appliances** where normal corrective appliances cannot be used or the result of a test indicates the need for them.

◆ To provide adequate **training and information** relating to the use of any workstations.

The Schedule covers the equipment (display screen, keyboard, work desk or surface, work chair), work environment (space, lighting, reflections and glare, noise, heat, radiation, humidity), and interface between computer and operator/user (suitability, ease of use and adaptability of software, provision of feedback to operators/users, format arrangements, software ergonomic applications).

Note: There are overlaps between these Regulations and the **Workplace (Health, Safety and Welfare) Regulations 1992, Electricity at Work Regulations 1989, Provision and Use of Work Equipment Regulations 1998, Management of Health and Safety at Work Regulations 1999**, etc.

HEALTH AND SAFETY (FIRST-AID) REGULATIONS 1981 AS AMENDED (SI 1981 NO. 917)

First aid is defined as meaning:

◆ In cases where a person will need help from a medical practitioner or nurse, treatment for the purpose of preserving life and minimising the consequences of injury or illness until such help is obtained.

◆ Treatment of minor injuries that would otherwise receive no treatment or do not need treatment by a medical practitioner or nurse.

There is a duty on the employer to:

◆ Ensure provision of facilities that are easily **accessible** to stretchers and any other equipment needed to convey patients to and from the first-aid room.

◆ Provide equipment which is **adequate and appropriate** for enabling first-aid to be rendered to employees.

◆ Inform employees of first-aid arrangements and sign-post facilities in compliance with the **Health and Safety (Safety Signs and Signals) Regulations 1996.**

Self-employed persons must provide their own first-aid equipment.

The Approved Code of Practice (ACoP) and Guidance to the Regulations (L74) outlines the factors to be considered in assessing first-aid provision, namely:

◆ Size of the organisation (e.g. number of employees).

◆ Nature of the work and workplace hazards and risks.

◆ Nature of the workforce.

◆ The organisation's accident history.

◆ The needs of travelling, remote and lone workers.

◆ Work patterns.

◆ The distribution of the workforce.

◆ The remoteness of the site from emergency medical services.

◆ Employees working on shared or multi-occupied sites.

◆ Annual leave and other absences of first-aiders and appointed persons.

◆ First-aid provision for non-employees (not a legal requirement but recommended).

There is no prescribed number of first-aiders. As an example, HSE Guidance suggests that a small office environment (with less than 25 people) should at least have an appointed person. The same environment with 25-50 people should have a first-aider trained in emergency first aid at work. Cover for sickness, holidays and shifts will also be needed.

There should be at least one first-aid box, the suggested contents of which are listed in the ACoP.

HEALTH AND SAFETY INFORMATION FOR EMPLOYEES REGULATIONS 1989 AS AMENDED (SI 1989 NO. 682)

These Regulations require information relating to health, safety and welfare to be provided to employees by means of posters or leaflets in a form approved by the HSE. The 2009 Amendment Regulations introduced a new design, which replaced the previous version following a transition period of five years.

© RRC International

HEALTH AND SAFETY (SAFETY SIGNS AND SIGNALS) REGULATIONS 1996 AS AMENDED (SI 1996 NO. 341)

These Regulations implement the EU Safety Signs Directive.

Employers must use a safety sign whenever there is a risk to health and safety that cannot be avoided or properly controlled by other means.

Signs must contain a pictogram instead of relying solely on text. Unfamiliar signs must be explained to employees.

Fire safety signs and signals, including fire exit signs and fire alarms, are included in the Regulations.

Pipework containing dangerous substances must be marked, e.g. by fixing labels or signs at sampling and discharge points.

Small stores of dangerous substances must also be marked as above.

The Regulations cover hand signals and acoustic methods as well as static or illuminated signs.

HSE GUIDANCE NOTES

The HSE issues Guidance Notes, which have no legal status and are purely of an advisory nature, to supplement information in Approved Codes of Practice.

HSE Guidance Notes describe good practice. They are issued in six specific series:

◆ General Series (GS).

◆ Chemical Safety (CS).

◆ Environmental Hygiene (EH).

◆ Medical Series (MS).

◆ Plant and Machinery (PM).

◆ Health and Safety Guidance (HSG).

IET REGULATIONS (THE WIRING REGULATIONS)

These Regulations, produced by the Institution of Engineering and Technology as a code of best practice, establish safety standards for people who design and work with electrical installations, e.g. designers, installers, erectors and testers of both permanent and temporary installations. The title of the current version of the Regulations is *IET Wiring Regulations 17th Edition (BS 7671:2008 incorporating amendment number 3:2015)*.

They are designed to protect employees and people generally from the hazards associated with electricity, but apply only to installations operating at up to 1,000 volts ac.

The Regulations emphasise the need for sound standards of workmanship and the competence of operators, and the use of suitable and correct materials to the relevant standard/specification.

Relevant definitions include:

◆ **Extra-low voltage** - not exceeding 50 volts ac or 120 volts dc.

◆ **Low voltage** - exceeding extra-low but not over 1,000 volts ac or 1,500 volts dc between conductors, or 600 volts ac or 900 volts dc between conductors and earth.

Guidance is given on factors which installation designers must consider, including the purpose of the installation, any external influences, maintainability, maximum demand, the number of conductors, earthing arrangements, type of supply and possible future extensions to the installation.

Extensive guidance is provided on methods of protection against the risks of shock, fire, burns and excess current.

Selection and erection of equipment to ensure fitness for the purpose is an important feature of the Regulations.

Procedures for inspection and testing to ensure an installation is safe, including the necessity for undertaking tests in a certain order to identify faults before an installation is energised by the supply, are further incorporated in the Regulations.

© RRC International

The latest amendment to the Regulations (no. 3:2015) includes changes to the electrical condition report section and new requirements for mobile and transportable electrical units, consumer units (to safeguard them against the risk of fire that can be produced from the overheating of connections) and the installation of luminaires and light fittings.

The above should be read in conjunction with the **Electricity at Work Regulations 1989** (see earlier).

INFORMATION

The **Health and Safety at Work, etc. Act 1974 (HSWA)**, Section 2(2)(c), and most health and safety Regulations place a duty on employers and others to provide information. Under most Regulations, employers are also entitled to receive information from employees.

The giving of information is an important feature of the communication process, and may be by word of mouth, training activities, meetings or by the use of written information.

Employers must further provide employees with information about, for instance:

◆ The **performance and plans** of the undertaking.

◆ Any **organisational changes** which may affect employees.

◆ The hazards and precautions required, including signs, etc. under the **Health and Safety (Safety Signs and Signals) Regulations 1996**.

◆ **Management** policies and intentions.

◆ Results of **air monitoring** and **health surveillance**.

◆ Aspects of health and safety relating to **DSE workstations**.

◆ The requirements of certain Regulations, e.g. the **Ionising Radiations Regulations 1999**, **Health and Safety (Consultation with Employees) Regulations 1996** and **Management of Health and Safety at Work Regulations 1999**.

◆ **Risks to hearing** and the precautions necessary.

◆ Use of **PPE** and its **limitations**.

◆ The use of **work equipment**.

The **Health and Safety Information for Employees Regulations 1989, as amended,** require the display of a statutory poster.

INSURANCE

The **Employers' Liability (Compulsory Insurance) Act 1969** requires employers to insure against claims by employees suffering personal injury, damage or loss.

The certificate of insurance must be displayed conspicuously at the workplace. Since 1 October 2008 following Amendment Regulations, it may be displayed electronically but employees must have reasonable access to it.

It is standard practice to extend such a policy to provide insurance against public liability.

The employer must disclose all information to an insurer for the insurance to be valid.

The policy must be approved by virtue of the **Employers' Liability (Compulsory Insurance) General Regulations 1971** and both the policy and the certificate must be made available to an enforcement officer.

The policy must state that any person under a contract of service or apprenticeship who sustains injury, disease or death caused during the period of insurance and arising out of the course of employment will be covered for any legal liability on the part of the employer to pay compensation.

Under the **Employer's Liability (Defective Equipment) Act 1969** the employer is deemed liable where injury is caused by defective equipment provided by the employer for use in his business and the defect is attributable (wholly or in part) to the fault of a third party (e.g. a manufacturer).

Under the **Occupiers' Liability Act 1957** an occupier has a duty of care to lawful visitors, who may be contractual invitees present with express or implied permission, and this is extended by the **Occupiers' Liability Act 1984** to trespassers who are owed a duty of common humanity. It is wise to insure concerning this liability as well as negligence at common law.

IONISING RADIATIONS REGULATIONS 1999 (SI 1999 NO. 3232)

These Regulations supersede and consolidate the **Ionising Radiations Regulations 1985** and the **Ionising Radiations (Outside Workers) Regulations 1993**. They provide a framework for safe working practices involving the use of radioactive substances and sources of ionising radiation. They impose duties to protect employees and other persons against ionising radiation arising from work with radioactive substances and other sources of ionising radiation. They also impose duties on employees.

© RRC International

Restriction of exposure is to be achieved by means of engineering controls and design features that include shielding, ventilation, containment, etc., together with the provision and use of safety features and warning devices. The Regulations require that radiation employers consult radiation protection advisers (RPAs) in respect of certain specified matters, and that employers ensure that adequate information, instruction and training is given to employees and other persons.

Other duties on employers include:

◆ Provision of **safe systems of work** which restrict exposure.

◆ Provision of adequate and suitably maintained **PPE (including respiratory protective equipment)** for employees and others in controlled or supervised areas.

◆ Control over sealed sources and unsealed radioactive substances **held in the hand or directly manipulated by hand**.

◆ Ensuring that **dose limits** are imposed and not exceeded for employees or other persons by carrying out **dosimetry** and **medical surveillance**.

◆ Designation of **controlled areas** and **supervised areas**, and control over entry to such areas and remaining in them.

◆ Designation of **classified persons** for work in controlled areas.

◆ Appointment of and consultation with **RPAs** to provide guidance on observance of the Regulations.

◆ Making and setting down **written local rules** to ensure compliance with the Regulations, bringing them to the attention of all concerned and ensuring observance of them.

◆ Provision of appropriate **supervision** and appointment of **Radiation Protection Supervisors (RPSs)** in writing, where work need not be notified, to ensure compliance with the local rules.

◆ Provision of **information, instruction and training** for employees, other persons, classified persons and trainees, and women of child-bearing age.

◆ Arranging the control, accounting for, safe keeping and safe transporting and moving of radioactive substances.

◆ Provision and maintenance of **washing and changing facilities** for controlled areas.

◆ Ensuring provision of **PPE** and conformance of **RPE** to approved standards in both cases.

- Ensuring **radiation monitoring** of controlled or supervised areas, providing and maintaining **monitoring equipment**, ensuring tests and examinations are carried out, and are under the supervision of a **qualified person**, and making and keeping suitable **records** for at least two years of such monitoring.

- Prior **assessment** of radiation hazards with a view to preventing accidents, occurrences or incidents, including **special hazard assessments** and the preparation of **reports**.

- Preparation of **contingency plans** in respect of any reasonably foreseeable accident, occurrence or incident.

- **Investigation** of exposure to ionising radiation to the extent that three-tenths of the annual **whole body dose limit** is exceeded.

- Ensuring **health surveillance records** are kept for at least 50 years.

- **Notification** of certain occurrences to the HSE without delay.

- Ensuring any equipment or apparatus used in connection with **medical exposure** is of such design or construction and is so installed and maintained as to be capable of restricting the exposure to ionising radiation when undergoing medical exposure to the extent that is compatible with the clinical purpose or research objective in view.

- **Investigation** of any incident where a person has been overexposed as a result of malfunction or defect in radiation equipment, and notification to the HSE where appropriate.

Duties of employees include:

- Not knowingly exposing themselves or others to ionising radiation to any extent greater than is reasonably necessary for the purposes of their work.

- Exercising reasonable care while undertaking such work.

- Making full and proper use of any PPE.

- Reporting defects in PPE immediately to their employer.

Duties are largely of a reasonably practicable nature.

© RRC International

JUDICIAL PRECEDENT

Decisions made by judges, or 'precedents', have a certain authority in the legal system.

Most precedents are binding precedents, meaning that the principle of law established in a former decision will be binding in subsequent cases founded on similar facts in courts of equal or lower rank. Precedents may be authoritative or persuasive:

◆ **Authoritative (or binding) precedents** are decisions which judges are bound to follow; a lower court is generally bound by a previous decision of a higher court.

◆ **Persuasive precedents** are decisions which are not binding upon a court, but which a judge may take into consideration (e.g. Judicial Committee cases, Commonwealth cases, USA cases, etc.).

Note: Not all judicial decisions set precedents.

(See also **CASE LAW** and **COMMON LAW**.)

L

LEGAL AID, SENTENCING AND PUNISHMENT OF OFFENDERS ACT 2012

This Act makes provision for a range of issues including legal aid, litigation funding, sentencing and punishment of offenders. Of particular interest to those involved in management of health and safety at work is the content of Section 85, which extends magistrates' sentencing powers in England and Wales.

Section 85 removes the cap on fines imposed in the magistrates' court on summary conviction.

LIFTING OPERATIONS AND LIFTING EQUIPMENT REGULATIONS 1998 (LOLER) AS AMENDED (SI 1998 NO. 2307)

These are consolidating Regulations replacing the **Construction (Lifting Operations) Regulations 1961**; Factories Act 1961, Ss. 21-27; **Offices, Shops and Railway Premises (Hoists and Lifts) Regulations 1968**.

Lifting equipment is defined as "equipment for lifting or lowering loads; it includes supporting, anchoring and fixing attachments". A load may be anything, including people.

The **Provision and Use of Work Equipment Regulations 1998** apply to guarding, maintenance and control systems. **LOLER** deals specifically with risks from load lifting.

Lifting equipment must:

◆ Be of **adequate strength and stability,** as must the load itself.

◆ Be designed to prevent falls, crushing, trapping or striking if used for lifting people.

◆ Be positioned and installed so as to prevent load drifting, free falling or unintentional release from causing injury.

◆ Have Safe Working Load (SWL) and other necessary safe use information marked on it.

◆ Be thoroughly **examined** after installation and prior to service.

◆ Have **defects** reported to the employer with Schedule 1 particulars.

◆ Not be used until defects are remedied.

◆ Have associated **information** as specified.

© RRC International

Lifting operations must be properly planned, organised, supervised and carried out safely.

Associated Approved Codes of Practice and Guidance Notes help compliance.

M

MACHINERY HAZARDS

See under **PROVISION AND USE OF WORK EQUIPMENT REGULATIONS 1998** later.

MANAGEMENT OF HEALTH AND SAFETY AT WORK REGULATIONS 1999 AS AMENDED (SI 1999 NO. 3242)

Absolute duties on an employer are:

◆ To make a suitable and sufficient assessment of the **risks to his own employees and other persons affected by his activities** in order to identify the measures he needs to take to comply with the requirements and prohibitions imposed on him by or under the **relevant statutory provisions.** (Similar provisions apply in the case of self-employed persons.) **(Reg. 3(1))**

◆ To **review and revise** risk assessments, and implement changes where necessary (Reg. 3(3)).

◆ To implement preventative and protective measures in accordance with the principles of prevention laid down in Schedule 1 to the Regulations **(Reg. 4)**.

◆ To ensure the effective **planning, organisation, control, monitoring and review** of the preventive and protective measures **(Reg. 5)**.

◆ To provide appropriate **health surveillance (Reg. 6)**.

◆ To appoint one or more **competent persons** to assist him in complying with the relevant statutory provisions **(Reg. 7)**.

◆ To establish and, where necessary, give effect to procedures to be followed in the event of **serious or imminent danger**, and nominate **competent persons** to implement these procedures **(Reg. 8)**.

◆ To ensure the arrangement of necessary contacts with external services, particularly as regards first-aid, emergency medical care and rescue work **(Reg. 9)**.

◆ To provide employees with comprehensible and relevant information on:

  ▸ the risks identified by the assessment;

  ▸ the preventive and protective measures;

  ▸ the emergency procedures;

  ▸ the competent persons to implement the emergency procedures; and

  ▸ the risks associated with shared workplaces, where appropriate. **(Reg. 10)**

© RRC International

◆ Where a workplace is shared:

  ▸ To **co-operate** with other employers.

  ▸ To take all reasonable steps to **co-ordinate** safety procedures.

  ▸ To **inform** other employers concerned of the risks arising out of or in connection with his own undertaking **(Reg. 11)**.

◆ To provide **comprehensible information** to employers from an **outside undertaking** on the risks arising from his own undertaking and the measures he has taken to comply with the relevant statutory provisions **(Reg. 12)**.

◆ With regard to capabilities and training:

  ▸ To take into account **health and safety capabilities** of individuals when entrusting tasks to them **(Reg. 13(1))**.

  ▸ To ensure health and safety training of employees:

    – At the recruitment stage.

    – On being exposed to new or increased risks due to transfer, change of responsibility, introduction of new work equipment, change respecting existing work equipment, introduction of new technology, introduction of a new system of work or change respecting an existing system **(Reg. 13 (2))**.

  ▸ **Training** is to be repeated periodically, adapted to take account of new or changed risks, and to be undertaken during working hours **(Reg. 13(3))**.

Absolute duties on employees are:

◆ To use any machinery, equipment, dangerous substances, transport equipment, means of production or safety device in accordance with any training or instructions received.

◆ To report situations of serious or immediate danger and shortcomings in the employer's protection arrangements **(Reg. 14)**.

There is a duty on employers to provide temporary workers with comprehensible information on:

◆ Occupational qualifications or skills required for safe working.

◆ Any health surveillance required under the relevant statutory provisions **(Reg. 15)**.

Women of child-bearing age who give notice of pregnancy must be specifically risk-assessed under Regulation 3 for any hazards that may affect them or their babies. If necessary, working conditions should be altered or, if not reasonable, temporary suspension may be necessary (especially for night work if a doctor's certificate so advises) **(Regs 16, 17 and 18)**. (Added by virtue of **EU Pregnant Workers' Directive**.)

Young persons must be separately risk-assessed and must be protected against certain special hazards which may arise owing to lack of experience, awareness of risks or maturity **(Reg. 19)**.

There are possible exemption certificates in relation to defence **(Reg. 20)**.

Note that civil liability arising from breach of these Regulations (specifically Regulations 14 to 16) is limited to new mothers and pregnant workers (see **CIVIL LIABILITY - BREACH OF STATUTORY DUTY**).

MANUAL HANDLING OPERATIONS REGULATIONS 1992 (MHOR) AS AMENDED (SI 1992 NO. 2793)

Manual handling operations means any transporting or supporting of a load (including lifting, putting down, pushing, pulling, carrying or moving it) by hand or by bodily force. There is a general duty on employers to avoid the need for manual handling.

Where it is not reasonably practicable to avoid manual handling, the employer must:

◆ Make a **suitable and sufficient assessment** of all such manual handling operations at work that involve a risk of injury.

◆ Take steps to **reduce risk** to the lowest extent reasonably practicable.

◆ Provide indications of the **weight** of any load and, with **epicentric loads**, the heaviest side of such a load.

The assessment is to be reviewed if no longer valid or if there has been a significant change in the operations to which it relates, and where changes to the assessment are indicated such changes shall be made.

The following factors are to be taken into account, in determining whether operations involve risk:

◆ Physical suitability of employee.

◆ Clothing, footwear or other personal effects.

◆ Employee's knowledge and training.

© RRC International

◆ Risk assessment undertaken to comply with Regulation 3 of the **Management of Health and Safety at Work Regulations 1999**, including whether this identifies the employee as being especially at risk.

◆ Health surveillance.

There is a duty on employees to make full and proper use of any system of work provided by the employer to reduce risk of injury.

The factors to be considered in a manual handling risk assessment are:

◆ The tasks.

◆ The loads.

◆ The working environment.

◆ Individual capability.

◆ Other factors, such as the effect on posture when using/wearing PPE.

MISCONDUCT

Misconduct implies some forms of behaviour which are deemed unacceptable and which could result in disciplinary action:

◆ **Misconduct** is action which is deemed a **breach of rules** and which, while not sufficiently serious to merit instant or summary dismissal, would result in a **formal warning**, e.g. non-observance of safety procedures, persistent lateness.

◆ **Gross misconduct** is an act which is so serious as to amount to the employee "**smashing (or repudiating) the employment contract**", with the result that **dismissal without notice** is deemed appropriate, e.g. physical assault, fraudulent practices, theft of company property. Usually people are suspended so that an impartial hearing can be conducted before any firm judgment is made.

Company rules/disciplinary procedures should specify aspects of behaviour which constitute both forms of misconduct. Case law, however, will add to the categories.

N

NEGLIGENCE (LAW OF TORTS)

Negligence can be defined as a breach of the legal duty to exercise reasonable care towards others (*Donoghue v. Stevenson (1932)*); it consists of careless conduct leading to injury, damage or loss (*Lochgelly Iron & Coal Co. Ltd. v. M'Mullan (1934)*.

The existence of a **duty of care** owed by the defendant to the claimant and **breach** of that duty must be established by an injured employee (or others) before a civil claim for damages can be brought. *Wilsons and Clyde Coal Co. Ltd v. English (1938)* lays down employers' duties to employees, which are now implied into contracts of employment as well as giving rise to negligence actions.

NEIGHBOUR PRINCIPLE

In *Donoghue v. Stevenson (1932)* Lord Atkin pronounced as follows:

"...The rule that you are to love your neighbour becomes, in law, you must not injure your neighbour; and the lawyer's question, Who is my neighbour? receives a restricted reply. You must take reasonable care to avoid acts or omissions which you can reasonably foresee would be likely to injure your neighbour. Who then, in law, is my neighbour? The answer seems to be - persons who are so closely and directly affected by my act that I ought reasonably to have them in contemplation as being so affected when I am directing my mind to the acts or omissions which are called in question."

In *Commissioner for Railways v. McDermott (1967)* Lord Gardner explained the position thus with regard to occupation of premises:

*"Occupation of premises is a ground of liability and is not a ground of exemption from liability. It is a ground of liability because it gives some control over and knowledge of the state of the premises, and it is natural and right that the occupier should have some degree of responsibility for the safety of persons entering his premises with his permission..... there is **proximity** between the occupier and such persons and they are his **neighbours**. Thus arises a duty of care........"* **(the Neighbour Principle).**

© RRC International

NEW ROADS AND STREET WORKS ACT 1991

The purposes of this Act are:

◆ To amend the procedures by which tolled roads are authorised, and make other provisions for the financing of roads by the private sector.

◆ To reform the legislation on street works by utility companies.

It repeals the **Public Utilities Street Works Act 1950** and amends other legislation.

NUISANCE (COMMON LAW)

Nuisance falls within the law of torts.

A common law **private nuisance** is one which apart from statute violates the principles which the common law lays down for the protection of individuals in the use and/or enjoyment of their rights over land.

A **public nuisance** at common law has been defined as an act not warranted by law, or an omission to discharge a legal duty, which act or omission obstructs or causes inconvenience or damage to the public in the exercise of rights common to all Her Majesty's subjects. Public nuisance may amount to a criminal offence as well as a tort in civil law.

Nuisances at common law may be private nuisances or public nuisances.

◆ **Private nuisances** can take many forms but, in all cases, they constitute some form of act, or failure to act, on the part of an individual or group that results in obstruction, inconvenience or damage to another individual or group in relation to land use/enjoyment.

  Actions in respect of private nuisance may take the form of a personal claim for damages and/or obtaining an injunction.

◆ **Public nuisances** have a direct effect on the public at large, such as obstruction of a public right of way.

  Actions in respect of public nuisances can be initiated by the Attorney-General, an individual or a local authority.

NUISANCES (STATUTORY)

These are covered in Part III of the **Environmental Protection Act 1990 (EPA)** (as amended by the **Clean Neighbourhoods and Environment Act 2005** and **Noise and Statutory Nuisance Act 1993**) and in Scotland by the **Environment Act 1995**, and are:

◆ any **premises** in such a state; or

- ◆ **smoke** emitted from premises; or

- ◆ **fumes or gases** emitted from premises; or

- ◆ any **dust, steam, smell or other effluent** arising on industrial, trade or business premises; or

- ◆ any **accumulation or deposit**; or

- ◆ any **animal** kept in a place or manner; or

- ◆ **noise emitted from premises**; or

- ◆ **noise emitted from vehicles, machinery or equipment in a street**; or

- ◆ **insects** emanating from any industrial, trade or business premises; or

- ◆ **artificial light** from premises;

that are prejudicial to health or cause a nuisance; and **any other matter** that is declared by any enactment to be a statutory nuisance.

Local authorities (LAs) have a duty to inspect an area from time to time to detect statutory nuisances and investigate complaints. Where the LA is satisfied as to the existence of a statutory nuisance, it may serve an abatement notice requiring the abatement of the nuisance and/or execution of works.

There is a right of appeal to a Magistrates' Court within 21 days on service of notice.

Failure to comply can result in:

- ◆ An unlimited fine plus a daily fine of up to one-tenth of the greater of £5,000 or level 4 on the standard scale (currently £2,500).

- ◆ For noise from industrial or trade premises an unlimited fine (£40,000 in Scotland).

The defence of best practicable means is available to a person charged.

An LA can undertake work in default and recover costs.

Action to abate a nuisance may also be taken by an individual through the Magistrates' Court (Sheriff Court in Scotland).

An abatement order can be made in respect of premises unfit for human habitation through the existence of a statutory nuisance.

© RRC International

O

OCCUPIERS' DUTIES (HSWA)

Duties of occupiers of non-domestic premises to non-employees who use such premises as a place of work or as a place where they may use plant or substances provided for their use there, are such that any person in control of the premises is to ensure that the premises, means of access/egress and plant and substances are safe and without risks to health. Duties also cover repair and maintenance of the premises (S.4, **Health and Safety at Work, etc. Act 1974**) (criminal law).

OCCUPIERS' LIABILITY ACTS (OLA)

Occupiers' liability in civil law is concerned with the duties of people and organisations who occupy land and premises, whose land and premises are visited by people for a variety of purposes.

In *Commissioner for Railways v. McDermott (1967)* Lord Gardner explained the position at common law (see **NEIGHBOUR PRINCIPLE** earlier).

There have been a number of amendments to the law relating to the liability of occupiers of premises for injury to persons and damage of property, namely the **Occupiers' Liability Acts 1957 and 1984**.

The **Occupiers' Liability Act 1957** established a common duty of care to all lawful visitors, namely a duty to take such care as in all the circumstances of the case is reasonable to see that the visitor will be reasonably safe in using the premises for the purposes for which he is invited or permitted by the occupier to be there.

Section 1 of the **OLA 1957** defines the duty of occupiers to all persons lawfully on the premises in respect of dangers due to the state of the premises or to things done or omitted to be done on them. Such liability is not confined to buildings and has been held to include, for instance, that of the main contractors retaining general control over a tunnel being constructed (*Bunker v. Charles Brand & Son (1969)*).

Visitors to premises are classed as including both invitees and licensees.

Protection is afforded to all lawful visitors, whether they enter for the occupier's benefit, such as customers, or for their own benefit, such as an enforcement officer, though not to persons exercising a public or private right of way over premises.

A possible way of limiting liability under the **OLA 1957** is the erection of warning notices, but a warning notice does not in itself absolve the occupier from liability unless in all the circumstances it is sufficient to enable the visitor to be reasonably safe.

An occupier must be prepared for children to be less careful than adults and must be aware of any lure or attraction to children, such as a pond, that could constitute a trap or allurement.

The **OLA 1984** imposes a duty of common humanity on the occupier in respect of trespassers. The **OLA 1984** defines trespassers as persons who may have lawful authority to be in the vicinity or not, who may be at risk of injury on the occupier's premises. (See **TRESPASS** later.)

The above duty can be discharged by issuing some form of warning, such as the display of a notice, but such a notice must be very explicit and its requirements actively enforced by the occupier. Hidden traps, etc. must not be used.

© RRC International

P

PERSONAL PROTECTIVE EQUIPMENT (PPE) AT WORK REGULATIONS 1992 AS AMENDED (SI 1992 NO. 2966)

The **Personal Protective Equipment at Work Regulations 1992** revoked much of the older, more specific PPE-related regulations and covered all protective equipment for use at work from protective clothing to footwear, eye protection, safety harnesses and respirators. There have been a number of amendments, including the **Health and Safety (Miscellaneous Amendments) Regulations 2002** which specified that PPE be assessed as being compatible with other PPE in simultaneous use and that, where necessary, PPE be used solely by the person to whom it is provided to limit risk and maintain a high level of hygiene.

The **PPE Regulations** do not apply where there is a more comprehensive requirement for provision and use of PPE, e.g. under the:

◆ Control of Lead at Work Regulations 2002.

◆ Ionising Radiations Regulations 1999.

◆ Control of Asbestos Regulations 2012.

◆ Control of Noise at Work Regulations 2005.

◆ Control of Substances Hazardous to Health Regulations 2002.

Personal protective equipment means all equipment (including clothing affording protection against the weather) which is intended to be worn or held by a person at work and which protects him against one or more risks to his health and safety, and any addition or accessory designed to meet this objective.

All PPE must comply with EU directives and standards.

There is a duty on the employer to ensure that PPE is suitable, namely that it:

◆ Is **appropriate** for the risks and conditions where exposure may occur.

◆ Takes account of **ergonomic requirements** and the **state of health** of the wearer.

◆ Is capable of **fitting** the wearer correctly.

◆ So far as is practicable, is **effective** in preventing or adequately controlling the risks without increasing the overall risk.

Where employees use more than one item of PPE simultaneously, such equipment must be compatible and continue to be effective.

Other requirements:

◆ The employer to assess the suitability of PPE at the selection stage and review the assessment if it is no longer valid or where there is a significant change in the matters to which it relates. The assessment must take account of ergonomic requirements, the state of health of the wearer, and the characteristics of the workstation.

◆ The employer to maintain the PPE in an efficient state, in efficient working order and in good repair, including the replacement and cleaning of PPE.

◆ Appropriate accommodation to be provided for storage of PPE when not in use.

◆ The employer to provide adequate and appropriate information to employees on the risks the PPE will avoid or limit, the purpose for and manner in which it is to be used, and any action to be taken by employees to ensure that it remains in an efficient state, in efficient working order and in good repair.

◆ The information provided to be comprehensible to the persons concerned.

◆ Employers to take all reasonable steps to ensure that the PPE is properly used.

Employees must:

◆ **Use** PPE in accordance with any training and instructions received.

◆ Ensure the PPE is returned to the **accommodation** provided.

◆ **Report** any loss or obvious defect straight away.

PRESSURE SYSTEMS SAFETY REGULATIONS 2000 (SI 2000 NO. 128)

These Regulations impose safety requirements with respect to pressure systems, although Transportable Gas Containers (TGCs) are covered by the **Carriage of Dangerous Goods and Use of Transportable Pressure Equipment Regulations 2009**.

The majority of duties are of an absolute nature.

'Pressure system' means:

◆ a system comprising one or more pressure vessels of rigid construction, any associated pipework and protective devices;

◆ the pipework with its protective devices to which a transportable pressure receptacle is, or is intended to be, connected; or

◆ a pipeline and its protective devices;

© RRC International

which contains or is liable to contain a relevant fluid, but does not include a transportable pressure receptacle.

A 'transportable pressure receptacle' means any container, other than an aerosol, used for the carriage of gas where the gas volume does not exceed 1,000 litres in seamed receptacles or 5,000 litres in seamless receptacles.

'Relevant fluid' means:

◆ **Steam**.

◆ Any **fluid or mixture of fluids** that is at a pressure greater than 0.5 bar above atmospheric pressure, and that is:

  ▸ A gas.

  ▸ A liquid that would have a vapour pressure greater than 0.5 bar above atmospheric pressure when in equilibrium with its vapour at either the actual temperature of the liquid or 17.5°C.

◆ A **gas** dissolved under pressure in a solvent contained in a porous substance at ambient temperature and that could be released from the solvent without the application of heat.

There is a general duty on designers, manufacturers, etc. to ensure that any pressure system or TGC:

◆ Is properly designed and constructed from **suitable material**.

◆ Offers **safe access** to the interior of the system without danger.

◆ Is provided with **protection devices**, and any such device which is designed to release contents does so safely, so far as is practicable.

Other requirements:

◆ Designers and suppliers of pressure systems to provide information on their design, construction, examination, operation and maintenance.

◆ Manufacturers to mark pressure systems with specified information.

◆ Installers to ensure that nothing about the way that a pressure system is installed gives rise to danger or impairs the operation of a protective device or inspection facility.

◆ Users of installed systems and owners of mobile systems (users and owners) to establish the safe operating limits of the systems.

◆ Users and owners must have a written scheme for the periodic examination, by a competent person, of the following parts of the system:

  ‣ All protective devices.

  ‣ Every pressure vessel and every pipeline in which a defect may give rise to danger.

  ‣ Those parts of the pipework in which a defect may give rise to danger.

  Such parts to be identified in the scheme.

◆ The user or owner to ensure that the:

  ‣ Scheme is drawn up or certified as suitable by a competent person.

  ‣ Content is reviewed at appropriate intervals by a competent person.

  ‣ Content is modified in accordance with recommendations of the competent person.

◆ The scheme to be suitable and should:

  ‣ Specify the nature and frequency of examination.

  ‣ Include measures necessary to prepare the system for examination.

  ‣ Where appropriate, provide for an examination to be carried out before the system is used for the first time.

◆ Examinations to be carried out in accordance with a written scheme of examination.

◆ Where the competent person identifies the potential for serious and imminent danger, unless certain repairs or modifications or changes to operating conditions are implemented, he shall make a written report straight away and, within 14 days, send a written report to the enforcing authority containing the same particulars.

◆ The user or owner to provide operators with suitable instructions on the safe operation of the system and action to be taken in an emergency.

◆ Systems to be properly maintained and in good repair, so as to prevent danger.

◆ There are specific requirements for record-keeping in respect of installed and mobile systems.

◆ The user of a pressure vessel to which Part IV applies shall ensure that the outlet is kept open and free from obstruction at all times.

◆ No person to supply for the first time, import, manufacture and use a TGC unless it meets certain conditions, namely:

  ‣ **Verification** by certificate as conforming to HSE-approved design standard/specification.

© RRC International

- ▸ There is an EU Verification Certificate in force.

- ▸ It bears **marks and inscriptions** required by the Framework Directive and the separate Directive relating to that kind of cylinder.

◆ The employer of a person who fills a TGC to check examination marks on the cylinder, its suitability for containing the relevant fluid, and make other appropriate safety checks, i.e. within safe operating limits, not overfilled and excess fluid removed.

◆ Owners of TGCs to ensure their examination at regular intervals and competent persons examining them to mark them with the date of examination.

◆ No person at work to modify a TGC of seamless construction, or that has contained acetylene, such that it is put outside the scope of the design standard or specification.

◆ No modified TGC to be supplied unless it is marked or certified as being fit for use. (There are similar provisions in the case of repaired TGCs.)

◆ Any person who rerates a TGC must be competent to do so and do it in accordance with written procedures drawn up by the owner.

◆ No person to supply a TGC that has been rerated unless it is certified as safe for use by an HSE-approved body.

◆ Specific provisions relating to records of TGCs to be kept by manufacturers, agents, importers and owners.

Two defences are available under the Regulations:

◆ **Act or default of another person**.

◆ **All reasonable precautions and all due diligence**.

The marking of pressure vessels is covered in Part IV. Information required includes:

◆ Manufacturer's name.

◆ Serial number.

◆ Date of manufacture.

◆ Standard to which the vessel was built.

◆ Maximum design pressure of the vessel.

◆ Maximum design pressure of the vessel where it is other than atmospheric.

◆ The design temperature.

PROVISION AND USE OF WORK EQUIPMENT REGULATIONS 1998 (PUWER) AS AMENDED (SI 1998 NO. 2306)

Work equipment includes any machinery, appliance, apparatus or tool and any assembly of components that, in order to achieve a common end, are arranged and controlled so that they function as a whole. Mobile work equipment (MWE) is also covered, including minimising risks of overturning by design or roll-over protection systems. Lifting equipment is also included but the **Lifting Operations and Lifting Equipment Regulations 1998** (see earlier) additionally apply. Lift trucks are included.

A related piece of legislation is the **Supply of Machinery (Safety) Regulations 2008**.

Other overlapping Regulations include:

◆ **Electricity at Work Regulations 1989.**

◆ **Control of Noise at Work Regulations 2005.**

◆ **Control of Substances Hazardous to Health Regulations 2002.**

Use means any activity involving work equipment, including starting, stopping, programming, setting, transporting, repairing, modifying, maintaining, servicing and cleaning.

Duties on employers and self-employed persons are largely of an absolute nature.

Employers to:

◆ Ensure work equipment is **constructed or adapted** so as to be **suitable** for the purpose for which it is used or provided.

◆ In **selecting** work equipment, consider the working conditions, and risks to health and safety in the premises or undertaking, as well as any additional risk in using the equipment.

They shall also ensure that:

◆ The work equipment is used only for those **operations** and under **conditions** for which it is **suitable**.

◆ The work equipment is **maintained** in an efficient state, in efficient working order and in good repair.

◆ Work equipment is inspected, including:

  ▸ Initial inspections to avoid incorrect installations giving rise to risks.

  ▸ Routine inspections where deterioration or exceptional circumstances may give rise to a risk.

© RRC International

▸ Keeping inspection records.

▸ Keeping inspection logs for relocated equipment.

▸ Evidence of last inspection for hired or borrowed equipment before use.

◆ The use of certain equipment which poses a **specific risk** is **restricted** to those given the task of using it, and repairs, modifications, maintenance or servicing are restricted to **designated persons.**

◆ **Designated persons** are adequately trained for this purpose.

◆ All those who use work equipment have adequate **information, instruction and training**, plus **written instructions** on correct use, foreseeable abnormal situations and action to be taken.

◆ Information and instructions are **readily comprehensible**.

◆ **Supervisors or managers** have received similar adequate training.

◆ **Listed measures** are taken to **prevent access** to any dangerous part of the machinery or to **stop the movement** of it before any part of a person enters a **danger zone**.

Regulation 11(2) gives a hierarchy of measures which should be taken, i.e. providing:

◆ Fixed guards.

◆ Other guards or protective devices.

◆ Jigs, holders, push-sticks or similar devices, used in conjunction with machinery.

◆ Information, instruction, training and supervision.

Guards and protection devices shall:

◆ Be **suitable** for the purpose.

◆ Be of good construction, sound material and adequate strength.

◆ Be **maintained** in an efficient state, in efficient working order and in good repair.

◆ Not give rise to **increased risks**.

◆ Not be easily bypassed or disabled.

◆ Be situated at a **sufficient distance** from a danger zone.

◆ Not unduly restrict the view of the operating cycle.

◆ Be so **constructed or adapted** that they allow operations or maintenance to be undertaken, but restrict access **only to the work area** and, if possible, without having to **dismantle** the guard or protection device.

There is a general duty on the employer to ensure that exposure of a person to specified hazards is either prevented or adequately controlled, such measures to be other than the provision of PPE, information, instruction, training and supervision, so far as is reasonably practicable, and to include measures to minimise the effects as well as reduce the likelihood of the hazard occurring.

Hazards are:

◆ **Falls or ejections** of articles or substances from work equipment.

◆ **Rupture or disintegration** of parts of work equipment.

◆ Work equipment catching **fire or overheating**.

◆ Unintended or premature **discharges** from work equipment.

◆ Unintended or premature **explosion** of the equipment or article or substance produced, used or stored in it.

Other requirements:

◆ The employer to take specific precautions against hazards from equipment associated with high or very low temperature.

◆ The employer to ensure adequate provision for:

  ▸ Controls for starting or making a significant change in operating conditions.

  ▸ Stop controls.

  ▸ Emergency stop controls.

  ▸ Controls (generally).

◆ The employer to ensure that:

  ▸ All **control systems**, so far as is reasonably practicable, are safe.

  ▸ Work equipment is provided with suitable means of **isolation** from sources of energy.

  ▸ **Reconnection** to energy sources does not expose any person to risk.

  ▸ Work equipment is stabilised by **clamping or otherwise**, where necessary.

  ▸ Suitable and sufficient **lighting** is provided in work equipment areas.

  ▸ **Maintenance operations** can, so far as is reasonably practicable, be undertaken when work equipment is shut down, or without risk to operators and with appropriate precautions being taken.

© RRC International

▸ Work equipment is **marked** in a clearly visible manner with appropriate markings, and incorporates appropriate **unambiguous, easily perceived and easily understood warnings given by warning devices**.

Risk of overturning of MWE should be minimised by design or the fitting of roll-over protection.

Self-propelled MWE must additionally include:

◆ Means of preventing seizure, or protective measures (especially of drive units or power take-off shafts).

◆ Measures to prevent unauthorised start-up.

◆ Braking, stopping and emergency braking systems.

◆ Self-contained lighting for low-light working.

◆ Mirrors, windows, etc. to improve driver viewing.

◆ Fire-fighting equipment where appropriate.

R

REACH

The EU Registration, Evaluation, Authorisation and Restriction of Chemicals Regulation (REACH) came into force on 1 June 2007, and replaces a number of European Directives and Regulations with a single system. It is being phased in over 11 years. It's a complicated subject that appeals mainly to specialists in the chemical industry but its purpose is to protect all of us and make industry more responsible for the chemicals they produce.

REACH has several aims:

◆ To provide a high level of protection of human health and the environment from the use of chemicals.

◆ To make the people who place chemicals on the market responsible for understanding and managing the risks associated with their use.

◆ To promote the use of alternative methods for the assessment of the hazardous properties of substances, rather than on animals.

A major part of REACH is the requirement for manufacturers or importers of substances to register them with a central European Chemicals Agency (ECHA). Enforcement in the UK is by the HSE which has been appointed as the 'Competent Authority'.

REACH applies to substances manufactured in or imported into the EU in quantities of one tonne per year or more. Generally, it applies to all individual chemical substances on their own, in mixtures or in articles (if the substance is intended to be released during normal and reasonably foreseeable conditions of use from an article).

Some substances are specifically excluded:

◆ Radioactive substances.

◆ Substances under Customs supervision.

◆ Substances being transported.

◆ Non-isolated intermediates.

◆ Waste.

◆ Some naturally occurring low-hazard substances.

© RRC International

Some substances, covered by more specific legislation, have tailored provisions, including:

◆ Human and veterinary medicines.

◆ Food and foodstuff additives.

◆ Plant protection products and biocides.

Other substances have tailored provisions within the **REACH** legislation, as long as they are used in specified conditions:

◆ Isolated intermediates.

◆ Substances used for research and development.

It is estimated that there are around 30,000 substances on the European Market in quantities of one tonne or more per year. Registering all of these at once would have been a huge task for both industry and regulators. To overcome this, the registration of those substances already being manufactured or supplied has been taking place in three phases spread over 11 years. To benefit from these phased-in deadlines, manufacturers or suppliers needed to pre-register their substances between 1 June and 30 November 2008. Pre-registration is not a legal requirement of **REACH** but was strongly advised by the UK Competent Authority.

Registration is a requirement on industry (manufacturers/importers) to collect and collate specified sets of information on the properties of those substances they manufacture or supply at or above one tonne per year. This information is used to perform an assessment of the hazards and risks that a substance may pose and how those risks can be controlled. This information and its assessment are submitted to ECHA in Helsinki.

The principle is that for any one substance, a single set of information on its intrinsic properties is produced by all those companies that manufacture or supply that substance working together in a Substance Information Exchange Forum (SIEF). Business-specific (e.g. company name) and business-sensitive (e.g. how it is used) information is submitted separately by each company.

In order to place on the market or use substances with properties that are deemed to be of "very high concern", industry must apply for an authorisation. A company wishing to market or use such a substance must submit an application to ECHA for an authorisation. Decisions on authorisation are made by the European Commission. Applicants will have to demonstrate that risks associated with uses of these substances are adequately controlled or that the socio-economic benefits of their use outweigh the risks. Applicants must also analyse whether there are safer suitable alternatives or technologies.

Safety data sheets now have to conform with slightly modified requirements set out in **REACH**.

REGULATORY REFORM (FIRE SAFETY) ORDER 2005 AS AMENDED (SI 2005 NO. 1541)

The **Regulatory Reform (Fire Safety) Order 2005 (RRFSO)** came into force on 1 October 2006. It applies to England and Wales only: the equivalent legislation in Scotland is the **Fire (Scotland) Act 2005 (Part 3)** and the **Fire Safety (Scotland) Regulations 2006**. Northern Ireland also has separate legislation.

The **RRFSO** replaces and consolidates a good deal of previous legislation. On introduction of the **RRFSO** the Fire Precautions Act 1971 was repealed and the **Fire Precautions (Workplace) Regulations 1997** were revoked, although many of the duties, including the requirement for fire risk assessment, were carried forward to the **RRFSO**.

The **RRFSO** simplified and reformed much of the previous legislation relating to fire safety in non-domestic premises, and placed a greater emphasis on fire prevention. The Order introduced significant changes in practice and affects both employers and fire authorities.

In essence, responsibility for fire safety inspection and risk assessment transferred from the fire service to the individual employer or responsible person(s). There is a greater emphasis on fire prevention in all non-domestic premises, including the voluntary sector and self-employed people with premises separate from their homes.

One of the most significant changes brought about by the introduction of the new legislation was the abolition of fire certification; fire certificates no longer have legal status. This includes the **Fire Certificates (Special Premises) Regulations 1976**. This represented a clear shift in responsibility for fire safety in the workplace away from the Fire and Rescue Services and onto employers and other persons in control of premises. The **Fire Safety and Safety of Places of Sport Act 1987** has been amended to avoid any conflict.

The duties that have been imposed on persons in control of premises as a result of, and in support of, this change include:

◆ The general duty to ensure, so far as is reasonably practicable, the safety of employees.

◆ The general duty in relation to non-employees to make such fire precautions as may reasonably be required in the circumstances to ensure that premises are safe.

◆ The duty to carry out a fire risk assessment.

© RRC International

Although this does involve a major shift of responsibility, the previous **Fire Precautions (Workplace) Regulations** already provided for a risk- assessment-based approach to fire safety in virtually all workplaces; and in premises where people are not employed to work, under existing health and safety legislation there were already duties of care requiring safety risks to be assessed, including the assessment of risk from fire. Hence the operator or owner of premises should already have been carrying out risk assessments, which include fire risks.

The Order makes a distinction between "**general**" fire precautions as required under the Order and "**special**" precautions which are necessary directly in connection with an industrial process and which fall under the scope of health and safety. The Order only covers general fire precautions and other fire safety duties which are necessary to protect relevant persons in case of fire in and around most premises. The Order requires fire precautions to be put in place where necessary and to the extent that it is reasonable and practicable in the circumstances of the case.

The **RRFSO** also introduced two important new terms:

◆ **Responsible person**: in a workplace this is the employer, if the workplace is to any extent under his control, and anyone else who may have control of any part of the premises, e.g. the owner, occupier or, in the case of shared workplaces, other employers.

◆ **Relevant persons**: any person who is, or may be, lawfully on the premises, and anyone in the immediate vicinity who is at risk from a fire on the premises.

Responsibility for complying with the **RRFSO** rests with the responsible person, i.e. the employer in a workplace and any other person who may have control of any part of the premises, e.g. the occupier or owner. In all other premises the person or people in control of the premises will be responsible. If there is more than one responsible person in any type of premises, all must take all reasonable steps to work with each other. The responsible person(s) must be identified. Except where a responsible person has sufficient training or knowledge he must appoint one or more competent persons to assist in undertaking preventive and protective measures under the Regulations.

Key requirements that must be addressed by all "responsible persons" include:

◆ The provision of **general fire precautions** to reduce the risk of fire and the risk of spread of fire.

◆ A suitable and sufficient **fire risk assessment** that addresses the risk of fire, and the risk of spread of fire, must be conducted. You must pay particular attention to those at special risk such as the disabled, and must include consideration of any dangerous substances likely to be on the premises. The fire risk assessment is intended to identify risks which can be eliminated or reduced and to decide the nature and extent of the general fire precautions required to protect people against the remaining fire risks. All significant findings must be recorded where five or more persons are employed.

◆ **Principles of prevention** - when implementing any preventive and protective measures the following principles should be adopted:

- ▸ Avoid risk.
- ▸ Evaluate risks which cannot be avoided.
- ▸ Combat risks at source.
- ▸ Adapt to technical progress.
- ▸ Replace the dangerous by the non-, or less, dangerous.
- ▸ Develop an overall prevention policy.
- ▸ Give priority to collective protective measures.
- ▸ Provide appropriate instruction for employees.

◆ The provision of **fire safety arrangements** - appropriate arrangements for the planning, organisation, control, monitoring and review of all fire safety arrangements must be developed and implemented.

◆ **Elimination or reduction of risks from dangerous substances** - to ensure that risks are either eliminated, or reduced so far as is reasonably practicable.

◆ **Fire-fighting and fire detection** - to ensure that, where necessary, appropriate equipment for detecting fire, raising the alarm and fighting fire is provided.

◆ **Emergency routes and exits** - to ensure, where necessary, that:

- ▸ Emergency routes and exits are kept clear at all times.
- ▸ Emergency routes lead directly to a place of safety.
- ▸ The number, distribution and dimensions of emergency routes and exits are adequate.
- ▸ Emergency doors open in the direction of escape, and can be opened easily by anyone in the event of an emergency.
- ▸ Emergency routes and exits are indicated by appropriate signs.
- ▸ Emergency routes and exits are provided with adequate emergency lighting.

© RRC International

◆ Establish **procedures for serious and imminent danger**, and nominate a sufficient number of competent people to help evacuate everyone from the premises.

◆ **Maintenance** - to ensure that the premises and any facilities or fire-safety equipment, etc. are adequately maintained, in efficient working order and good repair. All precautions provided must be subject to maintenance and must be installed and maintained by a competent person, who again must be identified. The precautions to be maintained include those provided for the use of the fire service in the event of fire, e.g. dry risers, etc.

◆ The provision of **safety assistance** - by the appointment of one or more competent persons to assist in the implementation of the fire-safety arrangements. Where an employer recognises that he may not have sufficient expertise to assess the risk in his premises, the fire service may be approached to provide suitable training.

◆ **Provision of information** - to employees, and the employers of any other persons working on the premises, with regard to the fire risks, the preventive and protective measures in force, and the emergency procedures.

◆ **Provision of training to employees on precautions and actions to be taken** in order to safeguard themselves and others. Training is to be given when first employed and also when exposed to new or increased risk. Refresher training should be given at suitable intervals.

◆ **Co-operation and co-ordination**. Where two or more responsible persons share, or have duties in respect of, premises they must take reasonable measures to:

  ▸ **Co-operate**, as far as is necessary, to enable compliance with the requirements of the **RRFSO**.

  ▸ **Co-ordinate** the preventive and protective measures they take.

  ▸ **Inform** the other responsible persons of the risks to relevant persons arising out of, or in connection with, their work activities.

The **enforcing authorities** for the **RRFSO** are:

◆ The **Fire Authority** - for the majority of workplaces and premises.

◆ The **Health and Safety Executive**:

  ▸ For nuclear installations.

  ▸ For ships, while under construction or repair.

  ▸ For construction sites.

◆ The **Local Authority** - for sports grounds.

© RRC International

The most common means of enforcement are by enforcement notices (equivalent to improvement notices) and prohibition notices. For the most serious offences prosecution is possible. In most, but not all, proceedings, it is a defence for the person charged to prove that he took all reasonable precautions and exercised all due diligence to avoid the commission of the offence. The exceptions for which this is not an acceptable defence are the duty to take general fire precautions, and measures to reduce or eliminate the risks from dangerous substances.

The enforcing authority may also issue an 'Alterations notice'. Where such a notice has been served, and before making changes to premises, services, fittings or equipment within the premises, or before increasing quantities of dangerous substances or changing the use of the premises, the responsible person must notify the enforcing authority of the proposed changes.

There are also specific arrangements for certain types of Crown and Defence Organisation premises.

REPORTING OF INJURIES, DISEASES AND DANGEROUS OCCURRENCES REGULATIONS 2013 (RIDDOR) AS AMENDED (SI 2013 NO. 1471)

These Regulations apply to events which arise out of or in connection with work, namely all deaths, certain injuries resulting from accidents, instances of specified diseases and defined dangerous occurrences.

Where any of the following events arise out of work activities, it must be notified by the quickest practicable means (e.g. telephone), and subsequently reported within 10 days (15 days for over-seven-day injuries) on the appropriate form, to the enforcing authority.

The events are:

◆ The **death** of **any person** as a result of a work-related accident, whether or not they are at work.

◆ Someone who is **at work** suffers a **specified injury** as a result of an accident.

◆ Someone who is **not at work** (e.g. a member of the public) suffers an **injury** as a result of a work-related accident and is taken from the scene to a **hospital for treatment**, or, **if the accident happens at a hospital**, suffers a **specified injury**.

◆ One of a list of specified **dangerous occurrences** takes place.

◆ Someone at work is unable to do their **normal work** for **more than seven days** as a result of an **injury** caused by an accident at work.

© RRC International

If a person dies, **within one year**, as a result of a reported injury, the employer is required to report this as soon as he is aware of it.

Cases of occupational disease should be reported as soon as the responsible person receives a diagnosis.

The duty to notify and report rests with the responsible person, i.e. the employer, a self-employed person or person in control of the premises.

Distributors and suppliers of gas must report incidents involving the use of their products and gas engineers must provide details of any gas appliances or fittings considered dangerous (possibility that people could die, lose consciousness or require hospital treatment).

A responsible person is to keep a record of the above events and also any accident if the worker has been incapacitated for more than three consecutive days.

There is a defence available for a person to prove that he was not aware of the event requiring him to notify or send a report to the relevant authority, and that he had taken all reasonable steps to have such events brought to his notice.

The list of 'specified injuries' (Regulation 4) includes:

◆ A fracture, other than to fingers, thumbs and toes.

◆ Amputation of an arm, hand, finger, thumb, leg, foot or toe.

◆ Permanent loss of sight or reduction of sight.

◆ Crush injuries leading to internal organ damage.

◆ Serious burns (covering more than 10% of the body, or damaging the eyes, respiratory system or other vital organs).

◆ Scalpings (separation of skin from the head) which require hospital treatment.

◆ Unconsciousness caused by head injury or asphyxia.

◆ Any other injury arising from working in an enclosed space, which leads to hypothermia, heat-induced illness or requires resuscitation or admittance to hospital for more than 24 hours.

The list of 'reportable occupational diseases' (Regulations 8 and 9) includes:

◆ Carpal tunnel syndrome where work involves regular use of percussive or vibrating tools.

◆ Severe cramp of the hand or forearm from prolonged periods of repetitive movement of the fingers, hand or arm.

◆ Occupational dermatitis from significant or regular exposure to a known skin sensitiser or irritant.

◆ Hand-arm vibration syndrome from regular use of percussive or vibrating tools or materials.

◆ Occupational asthma from significant or regular exposure to a known respiratory sensitiser.

◆ Tendonitis or tenosynovitis of the hand or forearm from work that is physically demanding and involves frequent, repetitive movements.

◆ Any occupational cancer.

◆ Any disease attributed to an occupational exposure to a biological agent.

There are 27 categories of dangerous occurrences (Schedule 2) that are relevant to most workplaces. Examples include:

◆ The collapse, overturning or failure of load-bearing parts of lifts and lifting equipment.

◆ Plant or equipment coming into contact with overhead power lines.

◆ The accidental release of any substance which could cause injury to any person.

Certain additional categories of dangerous occurrences apply to mines, quarries, offshore workplaces and certain transport systems (railways, etc.).

Reports are to be made on the following forms:

◆ F2508IE Report of an Injury.

◆ F2508DOE Report of a Dangerous Occurrence.

◆ OIR9BIE Report of an Injury Offshore.

◆ OIR9BDOE Report of a Dangerous Occurrence Offshore.

◆ F2508AE Report of a Case of Disease.

◆ F2508G1E Report of a Flammable Gas Incident.

◆ F2508G2E Report of a Dangerous Gas Fitting.

To make a report, complete the relevant form on the website at www.hse.gov.uk/riddor.

A telephone service can be used to report fatal and specified injuries only at the Incident Contact Centre on 0345 300 9923 (opening hours Monday to Friday 8.30 am to 5 pm).

© RRC International

RESTRICTION OF THE USE OF CERTAIN HAZARDOUS SUBSTANCES IN ELECTRICAL AND ELECTRONIC EQUIPMENT REGULATIONS 2012 (SI 2012 NO. 3032)

These Regulations implement Directive 2011/65/EU on the Restriction of the Use of Certain Hazardous Substances in Electrical and Electronic Equipment (EEE), and came into force on 2 January 2013. The objective of the Directive and Regulations is to contribute to the protection of human health, and to the environmentally sound recovery and disposal of waste electrical and electronic equipment.

The **RoHS Regulations** consist of four Parts and three Schedules.

RISK ASSESSMENT

The **Management of Health and Safety at Work Regulations 1999 (MHSWR)**, as amended, Regulation 3, places an absolute duty on an employer to undertake a suitable and sufficient assessment of:

◆ the risks to the health and safety of his **employees** to which they are exposed while they are at work; and

◆ the risks to the health and safety of **persons not in his employment** arising out of or in connection with the conduct by him of his undertaking;

for the purpose of identifying the **measures** he must take to comply with the requirements and prohibitions imposed upon him by or under **the relevant statutory provisions**.

A suitable and sufficient risk assessment should:

◆ Identify the **significant risks** arising out of the work.

◆ Enable the employer to **identify and prioritise** the measures that need to be taken to comply with the relevant statutory provisions.

◆ Be **appropriate** to the nature of the work and such that it remains **valid** for a reasonable period of time.

In particular, a risk assessment should:

◆ Ensure all relevant **hazards** are addressed and risk occurrence evaluated.

◆ Address what actually **happens** in the workplace or during the work activity.

◆ Ensure that all **groups** of employees and others who might be affected are considered.

◆ Identify groups of workers who may be **particularly at risk** (i.e. pregnant women and young persons must now be specifically risk- assessed (see **MHSWR**, Regulations 16 and 3(4) respectively)).

◆ Take account of existing preventive or precautionary measures.

The significant findings should include:

◆ The **significant hazards** identified in the assessment.

◆ The **existing control measures** in place and the **extent** to which they control the risks.

◆ The **population** which might be affected by these significant risks or hazards, including any groups of employees who are especially at risk.

All employers must undertake risk assessments.

Where five or more employees are employed, the assessment must be recorded in writing.

Current information such as HSE guidance, supplier instructions and information, trade press material, etc. should be taken account of in the process.

Employers should prioritise the necessary preventive and protective measures.

There are no fixed rules or procedures for risk assessments; the extent of the risk assessment will depend upon the relative complexity of the risks, processes involved, number of persons exposed, legal requirements and current safety procedures in operation.

A risk assessment will, in most cases, identify health and safety training needs and the need for information.

Where an assessment has been carried out under other Regulations, such as the **Control of Substances Hazardous to Health Regulations 2002**, it need not be repeated so long as it remains valid.

Where workplaces and work activities are standardised throughout an organisation, a model or generic risk assessment, applicable to these workplaces and/or activities, may be appropriate.

The process of risk assessment should be linked to duties outlined in the Statement of Health and Safety Policy and general duties under S.2, **Health and Safety at Work, etc. Act 1974**.

© RRC International

ROAD TRANSPORT

Legislation on the transport of dangerous substances is complex and reference should be made to the Regulations themselves for information. See the entry under **Carriage of Dangerous Goods and Use of Transportable Pressure Equipment Regulations 2009**.

S

SAFETY REPRESENTATIVES AND SAFETY COMMITTEES REGULATIONS 1977 (SRSC) AS AMENDED (SI 1977 NO. 500)

These Regulations are concerned with the appointment by recognised trade unions of Safety Representatives, the functions of Safety Representatives and the establishment and operation of Safety Committees. The Regulations are accompanied by an Approved Code of Practice and HSE guidance.

A recognised trade union may appoint Safety Representatives from among the employees.

The functions of Safety Representatives include:

◆ To **investigate** potential hazards and dangerous occurrences and examine the causes of accidents.

◆ To investigate health and safety **complaints** by the employees they represent.

◆ To make **representations** to the employer on matters arising from investigations.

◆ To make **representations** to the employer on **general matters** affecting health, safety and welfare.

◆ To carry out **inspections**.

◆ To **represent** employees in consultations with enforcement officers.

◆ To **receive information** from enforcement officers.

◆ To **attend meetings** of Safety Committees in their capacity as Safety Representatives in connection with the above functions.

◆ To be **consulted** by the employer on a range of health and safety issues.

Other provisions:

◆ The employer to permit Safety Representatives time off with pay during working hours for performing their functions and undergoing training.

◆ Safety Representatives are entitled to inspect the workplace after giving reasonable notice to the employer in writing and provided they have not inspected it within the last three months. They are further entitled to inspect the workplace where:

▸ There has been **substantial change** in the conditions of work.

© RRC International

> ‣ **New work equipment** has been installed by the employer.

> ‣ **New information** has been published by the HSE.

> ‣ There have been notifiable accidents, dangerous occurrences and diseases.

◆ The employer to provide facilities and assistance for inspections.

◆ Safety Representatives are entitled to inspect and take copies of documents relevant to the workplace that the employer is required to keep by virtue of any relevant statutory provisions, except the health records of an identifiable individual.

◆ The employer to make information available to enable Safety Representatives to fulfil their functions.

◆ Any two Safety Representatives can request, in writing, that the employer establishes a Safety Committee.

◆ The employer to consult with the Safety Representatives prior to the establishment of a Safety Committee and to post a notice stating the composition of the committee and workplaces to be covered by the committee.

◆ A Safety Committee to be established within three months of a request.

◆ Safety Representatives may complain to an employment tribunal where an employer has failed to permit time off and/or pay them.

SIMPLE PRESSURE VESSELS (SAFETY) REGULATIONS 2016 (SI 2016 NO. 1092)

These Regulations replaced the **Simple Pressure Vessels (Safety) Regulations 1991** in their entirety. They came into force on 8 December 2016 and apply to vessels placed on the market on or after that date.

For the purposes of these Regulations, 'vessel' means a simple pressure vessel manufactured in series with the following characteristics:

◆ welded, and intended to contain air or nitrogen at a gauge pressure greater than 0.5 bar, and not intended to be fired;

◆ made of certain types of steel or aluminium;

◆ cylindrical with outwardly dished or flat ends, or spherical;

◆ having a maximum working pressure not exceeding 30 bar, with the product of pressure and volume not exceeding 10,000 bar litres; and

◆ having a minimum working temperature no lower than -50°C, with a maximum working temperature no higher than 300°C if constructed of steel or 100°C if constructed of aluminium or aluminium alloy.

The Regulations place duties on manufacturers, importers and distributors and establish requirements for conformity, notification of conformity assessment bodies, market surveillance and enforcement. Essential Safety Requirements are given in Schedule 1.

Requirements on manufacturers of vessels with a stored energy of over 50 bar litres ('category A' vessels) include:

◆ Ensure that vessels meet the **essential safety requirements** with regard to design and manufacture.

◆ Draw up **technical documentation** and conduct/arrange for a **conformity assessment**. Manufacturers must keep this documentation, and the declaration of conformity, for 10 years from the day on which the vessel was placed on the market.

◆ Category A vessels must bear the **CE mark** and other specified inscriptions.

◆ Ensure that vessels are accompanied by **instructions and safety information**.

Requirements on manufacturers of vessels with a stored energy up to 50 bar litres ('category B' vessels) include:

◆ Ensure that the vessel has been designed and manufactured in accordance with sound engineering practice of a Member State.

◆ Category B vessels must bear specific **inscriptions** and other information referred to in regulation 11 (i.e. type and serial or batch identification, name or trade mark and address of manufacturer).

◆ Ensure that vessels are accompanied by instructions and safety information.

A manufacturer is also obliged to conduct sample testing of vessels it has manufactured and follow up complaints that vessels it has manufactured are not in conformity with Part 2 of these Regulations ('Obligations of economic operators'). Immediate corrective action (e.g. remedial work, withdrawal or recall) must be taken if vessels are found to not be in conformity with Part 2. Manufacturers must provide enforcing authorities with information and documentation when requested.

Vessels are categorised as follows:

◆ **Category A** - graded according to PS.V range: A1 - PS.V > 3,000 bar litres; A2 - PS.V >200 ≤ 3,000 bar litres; A3 - PS.V >50 ≤ 200 bar litres.

◆ **Category B** - vessels with PS.V of 50 bar litres or less.

© RRC International

SOCIAL ACTION, RESPONSIBILITY AND HEROISM ACT 2015

This Act sets out the issues to which a court must have regard in determining a claim in negligence or breach of statutory duty.

The court must have regard to:

◆ Whether the alleged negligence or breach of statutory duty occurred when the person was acting for the benefit of society or any of its members.

◆ Whether the person, in carrying out the activity in the course of which the alleged negligence or breach of statutory duty occurred, demonstrated a predominantly responsible approach towards protecting the safety or other interests of others.

◆ Whether the alleged negligence or breach of statutory duty occurred when the person was acting heroically by intervening in an emergency to assist an individual in danger.

STATEMENTS OF HEALTH AND SAFETY POLICY

There is a general duty under Section 2(3) of the **Health and Safety at Work, etc. Act 1974** for an employer to prepare and, as often as may be necessary, revise a written statement of his general policy with respect to the health and safety at work of his employees and the organisation and arrangements for the time being in force for carrying out that policy, and to bring the statement and any revision of it to the notice of his employees.

The Statement need not be written where fewer than five employees are employed.

The principal features of a Statement of Health and Safety Policy are:

◆ A **Statement of Intent** which outlines the organisation's overall philosophy in relation to the management of health and safety, including objectives for ensuring legal compliance.

◆ An **organisation** which should indicate the chain of command, accountability and responsibility for health and safety.

◆ **Arrangements** which detail the procedures and systems for monitoring performance and the overall implementation of the objectives detailed in the Statement of Intent including, for instance, the provision of information, instruction and training; risk assessment procedures; and accident reporting, recording and investigation procedures.

Many Statements incorporate sub-Statements such as those specifying a policy on sickness absence and training.

The **Management of Health and Safety at Work Regulations 1999** (see earlier) contain further detailed requirements as to Safety Policies.

STATUTES

Statutes (Acts of Parliament) are the written law produced through the Parliamentary process.

They override all other forms of law (except European Union law), and only Parliament can make, modify, repeal or amend statutes.

The stages in the making of a statute are:

◆ **First reading** - the **Bill's** short title is read by the Clerk of the House including the names of the members presenting and supporting it.

◆ **Second reading** - involves discussion of the Bill's principles; if it fails at this stage it cannot proceed any further.

◆ **Committee stage** - the Bill is subject to very close scrutiny and amendments are allowed at this stage. This usually takes place in a **Public Bill Committee** of between 16 and 50 MPs (formerly known as a Standing Committee) but may be taken in a **Committee of the Whole House.**

◆ **Report stage** - a formality if the Bill has not been amended at the Committee stage, and can move direct to the **third reading.** If the Bill has been amended at the Committee stage, the report stage provides an opportunity for MPs who were not on the Public Bill Committee to move amendments to, or reverse, the changes made at the Committee stage.

◆ **Third reading** - a formality if the Bill has got this far. If voted on favourably it is successfully passed through the **Commons procedure.**

◆ **House of Lords** - the Bill passes through a similar procedure. If the Lords wish to amend the Bill it is returned to the Commons for agreement. The House of Lords has only limited power to reject a Bill.

◆ **Royal Assent** - the last stage of the procedure. A Bill becomes an Act, although the implementation date may be postponed.

© RRC International

STRICT LIABILITY

Legal opinions can differ slightly on this but strict liability is generally where someone is held liable regardless of whether they were negligent (i.e. careless) or intended to do something. Thus, it is not necessary to prove negligence or wrongful intent for at least some aspects of the act for which the person is liable. In short, it is less about blame and more about establishing causation. The source of most strict liability is within statutes but some also exists in common law. It is a feature of both civil and criminal law.

◆ **Civil law** - a good example is Part I of the **Consumer Protection Act 1987**. This deals with product liability. In these cases, a producer is strictly liable if, on the balance of probabilities, a defect in a product causes death or injury or loss (of personal property). The injured person does not have to prove that the producer was negligent (the Act does, however, contain some specific defences).

◆ **Criminal law** - road traffic legislation has many examples of this as it would otherwise be difficult or very costly to enforce. For example, someone can be found guilty of speeding without having to prove that they intended to do so. Many health and safety and environmental pollution offences are also of this type. Once again, defences are usually stated in the relevant Act or regulation (e.g. 'Due Diligence' defence - see earlier).

The terms strict liability, absolute liability and no-fault liability are sometimes used interchangeably. Some distinguish between strict and absolute liability. For further reading on the (somewhat fine) legal distinction, see the Court of Appeal case: *Allison v. London Underground Ltd (2008) EWCA Civ 71* available at **www.bailii.org/ew/cases/EWCA/Civ/2008/71.html**

T

TORTS

A tort is a civil wrong. Principal torts relating to health and safety at work are those of negligence, nuisance and trespass. (See **NEGLIGENCE (LAW OF TORTS)**, **NUISANCE (COMMON LAW)** and **TRESPASS**.)

TRESPASS

Trespass falls within the law of torts and implies the intentional invasion of an individual's person, land or goods. It is actionable without proof of damage.

An action for trespass involves a civil claim for damages resulting from:

◆ false imprisonment and/or assault and/or battery (**trespass to the person**); or

◆ unlawful entry on to the land of another (**trespass to land**); or

◆ unlawful interference with goods (**trespass to goods**).

A trespasser to land is defined in common law as a person who:

◆ Goes on to premises without invitation or permission.

◆ Although invited or permitted to be on premises, goes to a part of the premises to which the invitation or permission does not extend.

◆ Remains on premises after the invitation or permission to be there has expired.

◆ Deposits goods on premises when not authorised to do so.

See also **OCCUPIERS' LIABILITY ACTS**.

© RRC International

UNFAIR CONTRACT TERMS ACT 1977

This Act states that a person cannot, by reference to any contract term or to a notice given to persons generally, exclude or restrict his liability for death or personal injury resulting from negligence.

It is unlawful to contract out of, or to seek to modify, liability for personal injury or death caused by negligence. Exclusion clauses are void.

As far as damage to property is concerned, whether by negligence or otherwise, the contract term must be fair and reasonable in the light of the circumstances at the time liability arose and under guidelines laid down in Schedule 2. Exclusion clauses are voidable.

Consumer rights under the **Sale of Goods Act 1979**, **Consumer Credit Act 1974** and **Supply of Goods and Services Act 1982** cannot be excluded.

UNFAIR DISMISSAL

This is concerned with whether a decision to dismiss an employee can be justified by the reasons given for the decision and the manner in which the dismissal is handled.

Dismissal occurs when:

◆ The employer **terminates** the employee's contract, with or without notice.

◆ The employee terminates the contract by **resigning** because of the employer's behaviour (**constructive dismissal**).

◆ The employer fails to renew a fixed-term contract of two years or more when it expires.

A fair dismissal is one which satisfies a two-stage test of fairness:

◆ It can be specified that the **reason for dismissal** is one of the following:

  ▶ Capability or qualifications of the employee.

  ▶ Conduct of the employee.

  ▶ Redundancy.

  ▶ Where continued employment would contravene some other statute or regulation.

  ▶ "Some other substantial reason".

◆ The employer acted **reasonably** in the circumstances (e.g. followed reasonable procedures).

If the employer cannot bring the dismissal within the above criteria it will be an unfair dismissal and an employee who has at least one year's continuous service (two years' continuous service for employees commencing employment on or after 6 April 2012) can claim compensation and possibly reinstatement in some cases via an employment tribunal. Cases must generally be brought within three months of dismissal.

Dismissal is automatically deemed unfair, regardless of length of service of the employee, where the following issues are concerned:

◆ Discrimination (sex, race or disability).

◆ Trade union membership or activities.

◆ Pregnancy or maternity.

◆ Asserting statutory employment rights (including the national minimum wage and working time).

◆ Asserting health and safety rights.

Age discrimination may also be a consideration.

Employees complaining of breach of contract (including wrongful dismissal) may sue in the County or High Court regardless of length of service.

© RRC International

V

VICARIOUS LIABILITY

Vicarious liability is based on the fact that if an employee, while acting in the course of his employment, negligently injures another employee or the employee of another employer, his employer will be jointly liable with him for that injury (see *Lister v. Romford Ice and Cold Storage Co. Ltd (1957)* and the Civil Liability (Contribution) Act 1978). Vicarious liability can also apply to other branches of law, including the criminal law and agency.

Vicarious liability usually rests on the employer simply as a result of the fact that he is the employer and is deemed to have ultimate control over his employees, i.e. the Master and Servant relationship.

This liability must be insured against under the **Employers' Liability (Compulsory Insurance) Act 1969**.

Employers cannot contract out of this liability as it is prohibited by the **Law Reform (Personal Injuries) Act 1948 and the Unfair Contract Terms Act 1977**.

An employee can be sued instead of, or as well as, his employer where the employee has been negligent (*Lister v. Romford Ice and Cold Storage Co. Ltd (1957)*).

W

WASTE ELECTRICAL AND ELECTRONIC EQUIPMENT REGULATIONS 2013 AS AMENDED (SI 2013 NO. 3113)

These Regulations (usually known as the **WEEE Regulations**) implement **Directive 2012/19/EU** on Waste Electrical and Electronic Equipment (WEEE). They are an example of 'Extended Producer Responsibility' which is implemented by a number of European Directives, the underlying principle being to require producers to take financial responsibility for the environmental impact of products they place on the market, particularly when these products become waste. The objectives of the **WEEE Directive** are ideally the prevention of WEEE, and in addition the re-use, recycling and other forms of recovery of such wastes so as to reduce the disposal of waste.

The **WEEE Regulations** consist of 14 Parts and 14 Schedules.

WORK AT HEIGHT REGULATIONS 2005 (SI 2005 NO. 735)

A place is at height if a person could be injured falling from it, even if it is at or below ground level. The employer must do all that is reasonably practicable to prevent anyone falling.

Duty holders must:

◆ Avoid work at height where they can.

◆ Use work equipment or other measures to prevent falls where they cannot avoid working at height.

◆ Where the risk of a fall cannot be eliminated, use work equipment or other measures to minimise the distance and consequences of a fall should one occur.

The Regulations require duty holders to ensure that:

◆ All work at height is properly planned and organised.

◆ All work at height takes account of weather conditions that could endanger health and safety.

◆ Those involved in work at height are trained and competent.

◆ The place where the work at height is done is safe.

◆ Equipment for work at height is appropriately inspected.

◆ The risks from fragile surfaces are properly controlled.

◆ The risks from falling objects are properly controlled.

© RRC International

WORKING TIME REGULATIONS 1998 (WTR) AS AMENDED (SI 1998 NO. 1833)

These Regulations (as amended) stipulate basic limits on working time and entitlement to periods of rest between working time, in-work breaks and to paid annual leave.

The basic rights and protections that the Regulations provide are:

◆ A limit of an average of 48 hours' work a week, which a worker can be **required** to work (though workers can **choose** to work more if they want to).

◆ A limit of an average of eight hours' work in 24 which night workers can be required to work.

◆ A right for night workers to receive free health assessments and a transfer to daytime working if there are health problems.

◆ A right to 11 hours' rest a day.

◆ A right to a day off each week.

◆ A right to an in-work rest break of at least 20 minutes if the working day is longer than six hours and adequate rest breaks for monotonous work.

◆ From April 2009, a right to 5.6 weeks' paid leave per year (inclusive of bank holidays).

The above applies to full-time, part-time, casual and temporary workers, etc. There are some exclusions. Complaint is to an employment tribunal if an employee is denied his/her rights.

In the UK an opt-out from the maximum working time has been in place for many years.

WORKPLACE (HEALTH, SAFETY AND WELFARE) REGULATIONS 1992 AS AMENDED (SI 1992 NO. 3004)

These Regulations have applied to all workplaces since 1 January 1996.

The duties on employers are largely of an absolute nature.

Workplace is defined as meaning any premises or part of a premises that are not domestic premises and which are made available to anyone as a place of work, including:

◆ any place within the premises to which such a person has access while at work; **and**

◆ any room, lobby, corridor, staircase, road or other place used as a means of access to or egress from the workplace or where facilities are provided for use in connection with the workplace other than a public road.

Certain workplaces are exempted, e.g. workplaces in or on a ship, construction operations, and mining operations.

There are general duties on employers and those in control of workplaces to comply.

The workplace, equipment, devices and systems are to be maintained (including cleaned as appropriate) in an efficient state, efficient working order and in good repair.

The Regulations cover three specific aspects of workplaces:

◆ Environmental working conditions.

◆ Structural safety.

◆ Welfare amenity provisions.

Requirements relating to environmental working conditions include:

◆ Maintenance of a **reasonable temperature** inside buildings.

◆ Provision of safe **heating appliances**.

◆ Provision of **thermometers**.

◆ Suitable and sufficient **lighting**.

◆ Maintenance of **cleanliness** and provision of **cleanable surfaces**.

◆ Control over **waste materials**.

◆ Prevention of **overcrowding**.

◆ Suitability of **workstations** and **seats**.

Requirements relating to structural safety include:

◆ Suitability and condition of **floors and traffic routes**.

◆ Prevention of **falls and falling objects**.

◆ **Structural and operational requirements** for windows and transparent or translucent doors, gates and walls; skylights and ventilators; escalators and moving walkways.

◆ Safe **window cleaning** arrangements.

© RRC International

Requirements relating to welfare amenity provisions include:

◆ Provision of suitable and sufficient **sanitary conveniences** and **washing facilities**.

◆ An adequate supply of wholesome **drinking water**.

◆ Accommodation for **clothing**.

◆ Facilities for **changing clothing**.

◆ Facilities for **rest** and to **eat meals**.

◆ Rest facilities for **pregnant women and nursing mothers**.

Schedule 1 covers provisions for 'old' factories with regard to space and the number of sanitary conveniences.

Y

YOUNG PERSONS AND CHILDREN

A **child** is a person under minimum school-leaving age, which, at present, is under 16 years.

A **young person** is someone who has ceased to be a child, but who is not yet 18 years old (i.e. 16 or 17 years of age).

Regulations 3(4) and 19 of the **Management of Health and Safety at Work Regulations 1999, as amended,** require a specific formal risk assessment prior to employment. The assessment must take into account inexperience and immaturity, and risks associated with those agents, processes and work listed in Regulation 19. Young persons are excluded from certain categories of work except under the supervision of a competent person.

The **Health and Safety (Training for Employment) Regulations 1990** apply the **Health and Safety at Work, etc. Act 1974 (HSWA)** to cover school pupils and college and university students on work experience and training courses for employment. The educational establishment is treated as being the 'employer' of the trainee and **HSWA** applies.

Other general statutory provisions include the **Employment of Women, Young Persons and Children Act 1920;** the **Children and Young Persons Acts 1933** and **1963, as amended** by the **Employment of Children Act 1973;** the **Children and Young Persons (Scotland) Act 1937;** the **Education Act 1996;** the **Children (Protection at Work) Regulations 1998;** the **National Minimum Wage Act 1998** and the **Working Time Regulations 1998.**

There are also specific restrictions and prohibitions associated with legislation covering:

◆ Agriculture.

◆ Dangerous machines.

◆ Lead.

◆ Potteries.

◆ Radiation.

◆ Woodworking machinery.

© RRC International

APPENDIX

TABLE OF KEY HEALTH AND SAFETY CASE LAW

Case	Description	Subject Area
Adsett v. K&L Steelfounders & Engineers Ltd (1953)	A foundry worker (Adsett) contracted pneumoconiosis while at work. Some time later, the employer, K&L, installed an extractor system, although this came too late to help Adsett. It was held that K&L were not liable for failing to provide extraction earlier as the system had not been invented.	The meaning of 'Practicable'.
Barber v. Somerset County Council (2004)	Barber was a teacher who worked up to 70 hours per week. He informed his employer that he was experiencing 'work overload' and eventually went sick with stress and depression. On return, he advised senior management that the situation was damaging his health. No help was forthcoming. B eventually retired on grounds of ill health. The House of Lords (whose appellate role is now fulfilled by the Supreme Court) found in favour of B. The senior management team should have helped him once they had become aware of his difficulties. Their failure to act led to his breakdown.	Employers' liability for work-related stress
British Railways Board v. Herrington (1972)	A six-year-old child, Herrington, wandered onto a rail track through a fence that the Board had not maintained. The House of Lords (whose appellate role is now fulfilled by the Supreme Court) held that the Board as occupiers of the railway premises owed a duty of care even to trespassers and this was extended in the **Occupiers' Liability Act 1984**.	Occupiers' liability to trespassers.
Caparo Industries Plc v. Dickman (1990)	This case established a three-stage test to see if a duty of care is owed by one party to another: 1. The harm suffered by the claimant must be reasonably foreseeable. 2. There should be sufficient proximity between claimant and defendant. 3. It must be fair, just and reasonable to impose such a duty.	Duty of care - establishing when a duty is owed.

Case	Description	Subject Area
Corr v. IBC Vehicles Ltd (2008)	Corr, a maintenance engineer employed by IBC, sustained head injuries in an accident at work. He suffered from post traumatic stress disorder and committed suicide almost 6 years later. Mrs Corr succeeded in a damages claim against IBC. IBC appealed, arguing amongst other things that the death was too remote from the original injury, that it fell outside their duty of care and that death was not reasonably foreseeable. The House of Lords (whose appellate role is now fulfilled by the Supreme Court) held that IBC owed Mr Corr a duty of care and that some damage was foreseeable due to Mr Corr's depression. The suicide did not break the chain of causation. IBC were held responsible.	Causation in negligence cases.
Donoghue v. Stevenson (1932)	Donoghue drank from a bottle of ginger beer with snail remains - after falling ill, she sued the manufacturers who argued that the retailer was responsible. The House of Lords (whose appellate role is now fulfilled by the Supreme Court) held that manufacturers had a duty of care to ensure bottled drink should not cause harm.	Neighbour principle and duty of care.
Edwards v. National Coal Board (1949)	Mine legislation required mine owners to take "reasonably practicable" steps to ensure that all travelling roads in coal mines were safe. A section of the road gave way, killing Edwards. The judge said that while a balance must be struck between likely risk of collapse and loss of life, and the cost of maintaining the road, in this case loss of life was not an insignificant risk and the road should have been made safe.	Reasonably practicable.

© RRC International

Case	Description	Subject Area
Fairchild v. Glenhaven Funeral Services Limited and Others (2002)	Where a claimant suffers mesothelioma after being negligently exposed to asbestos fibres during the course of employment with more than one employer, in circumstances where he could not prove which defendant's negligence was the cause of the disease, it is enough for the claimant to prove that a defendant materially increased the risk of injury. In such cases, the claimant will be able to recover damages from all those employers who materially contributed to the risk of the claimant developing mesothelioma. Each defendant would be liable in full for the claimant's damages.	Joint and several liability for damages in mesothelioma cases.
Intel Corp. (UK) Ltd v. Daw (2007)	Daw worked for Intel and had experienced an increase in workload, which led to a nervous breakdown. She sued in negligence. In their defence, Intel argued that they offered free counselling to staff who felt stressed. However, the House of Lords (whose appellate role is now fulfilled by the Supreme Court) held that the provision of counselling services alone was not 'a panacea by which employers can discharge their duty of care in all cases'. The provision of counselling services alone will therefore seldom be enough to discharge an employer's liability in relation to work-related stress.	Employers' liability for work-related stress - provision of counselling services.
J. Armour v. J. Skeen (Procurator Fiscal) (1977)	A workman fell to his death while repairing a bridge over the River Clyde. The director of roads for the regional Council, Armour, was responsible for supervising the safety of his road workers but had failed to produce a written safety policy. Accordingly, he was prosecuted under the **Health and Safety at Work, etc. Act 1974.**	Personal liability of executives. Application of **HSWA** s.37.
Jones v. Livox Quarries Ltd (1952)	Against instructions, Jones hitched a lift on the tow bar of one of the defendant's excavators. He was injured and sued in negligence. The Court of Appeal held that J, who had deliberately exposed himself to danger, was to some extent responsible for his injury. Contributory negligence was assessed at 20%.	Contributory negligence.

Case	Description	Subject Area
Latimer v. AEC Ltd (1953)	A factory floor was flooded and became slippery due to oil residue. In spite of sawdust covering, an employee slipped and was injured. Held: that the employer had taken reasonable steps to maintain the floor and prevent against slips under normal circumstances, and that heavy rainfall was unforeseeable.	Safe place of work. Practicability of precautions. Freak and unexpected hazard.
Marshall v. Gotham and Co. Ltd (1954)	A mine roof was tested but subsequently collapsed due to a rare geological fault. The judges decided that the employers had taken reasonable precautions and were therefore not liable. More precautions would be prohibitively expensive. Held: that where precautions are reasonable, they should be taken.	So far as is practicable.
Mersey Docks and Harbour Board v. Coggins and Griffiths (Liverpool) Ltd (1946)	C&G hired a crane driver and crane from Mersey Docks and Harbour Board (M). In working his crane the driver negligently injured one of C&G's employees. The outcome of the case turned on the question of whether the employer/employee relationship had passed from M to C&G. The House of Lords (whose appellate role is now fulfilled by the Supreme Court) decided that the test was "Who had the authority to direct or delegate to the workman the manner in which the vehicle was driven?" Here, in operating the crane, the driver was using his own discretion which had been delegated to him by his regular employer (M). If he made a mistake in operating the crane, this was nothing to do with C&G. The power to control the method of performing the work was not transferred from M to C&G, therefore M retained control over the driver and was vicariously liable for the driver's negligence.	Vicarious liability for a hired-out employee.

© RRC International

Case	Description	Subject Area
Mitchell and Others v. United Co-operatives Ltd (2012)	The claimant employees claimed for psychiatric injury suffered when the shop they worked in was robbed. Their claim failed at first instance and so they appealed. In dismissing the appeal, the Court of Appeal held that the employer's failure to install security screens and provide a full-time security guard at the shop did not amount to a failure to take reasonable care.	Employer's liability for psychiatric injury.
O'Toole v. First Quench (2005)	A court held that it would be unreasonable to 'double staff' purely as a deterrent against robberies.	Employer's duty to reduce risk of violence.
Paris v. Stepney Borough Council (1951)	A one-eyed garage worker became completely blinded after a chip of metal entered his good eye. He had been given no protective equipment. Mr Paris successfully claimed damages for his injury but this was overturned on appeal. He then appealed to the House of Lords (whose appellate role is now fulfilled by the Supreme Court). The House of Lords held that, where an employer is aware that an employee has a disability which, although it does not increase the risk of an accident occurring, does increase the risk of serious injury, special precautions should be taken if the employer is to fulfil its duty to take reasonable care for the safety of that employee. Stepney Borough Council owed a special duty of care to Mr Paris and had been negligent in failing to supply goggles to him, even though such equipment was not given to other employees.	Special duty of care owed to vulnerable persons.

Case	Description	Subject Area
R. v. Associated Octel Co. Ltd (1996)	Octel engaged contractors to repair a tank and issued a permit-to-work, although this was inadequate and unmonitored. A contractor's employee was subsequently injured in a flash fire inside the tank. HSE prosecuted Octel, who were fined £25,000. Octel appealed to the Court of Appeal, then the House of Lords (whose appellate role is now fulfilled by the Supreme Court). The House of Lords held that employers who engage contractors must, subject to reasonable practicability, ensure the contractor's health and safety. Tank repair was part of Octel's wider undertaking and so they were responsible for the safety of those doing the work. The appeal was dismissed.	HSWA s.3 - definition of 'undertaking'.
R. v. British Steel plc (1995)	British Steel (B) engaged sub-contractors to move a steel platform by crane. B provided all equipment, plus an engineer to supervise, Mr Crabb (C). During the operation, one of the workers was killed. When prosecuted, B argued that senior managers had taken all reasonable care in delegating supervision to C and that this was reasonably practicable. The judge held that the defence of 'proper delegation' did not arise and B was duly convicted. On appeal, the Court of Appeal held that s.3(1) imposes absolute liability subject to reasonably practicable measures to avert the risk. The appeal was dismissed. Corporations cannot avoid liability simply by delegating responsibility to someone other than the directing mind of the company.	HSWA s.3 - no defence of 'proper delegation'.
R. v. Chargot Ltd (2008)	In prosecutions for breaches of s.2(1) and/or s.3(1) **HSWA**, the prosecution has only to prove that the result described in those sections had not been achieved or prevented. It is then up to the defendant to show that they had done what was reasonably practicable in the circumstances. Prosecutors need to do more than simply assert that a state of affairs existed, although they do not have to identify and prove specific breaches of duty.	Standard of proof in prosecutions for breaches of ss.2 and 3 **HSWA**.

© RRC International

Case	Description	Subject Area
R. v. HTM (2006)	Following a fatal accident, HTM was prosecuted for breach of s 2(1) **HSWA**. To avoid conviction, HTM had to prove (on a balance of probabilities) that it would not be reasonably practicable to do more than they actually did (s.40 **HSWA**). The defendant argued that the accident would not have occurred if the employees had followed the safety instructions that had been provided and that their conduct could not have been foreseen. In a preparatory hearing, it was held that HTM, in asking the jury to consider whether it had established that it had done all that was reasonably practicable, could not be prevented from adducing evidence in support of its case that it had taken all reasonable steps to eliminate the likelihood of the relevant risk coming to pass.	**HSWA** s.2(1) - relevance of foreseeability.
R. v. Nelson Group Services (Maintenance) Ltd (1998)	The Court of Appeal stated that an isolated act of negligence by an employee carrying out work on behalf of the company does not stop that employer from establishing a defence that it has done everything that is reasonably practicable.	Reasonable practicability.
R. v. P (2007)	A child was being carried as a passenger on a forklift truck and was killed. The employer was prosecuted under s.3 **HSWA**. A company director, P, was charged under s.37(1) in that the offence committed by the company was committed with his consent or connivance or was attributable to neglect on his part. The Court of Appeal held that to establish neglect (in contrast to consent or connivance) it was necessary to establish "if there had not been actual knowledge of the relevant state of facts, nevertheless the officer of the company should have, by reason of the surrounding circumstances, been put on enquiry as to whether or not the appropriate safety procedures were in place. That would depend on the evidence in every case".	s.37 **HSWA** - meaning of 'neglect'.

Case	Description	Subject Area
R. v. Porter (2008)	Porter was headmaster of a school where a three-year-old sustained a head injury after jumping from a flight of steps. The trial judge held that it would be reasonably practicable to put in place constant supervision to prevent the child from descending the steps. Mr Porter was convicted of a breach of s.3(1) **HSWA** and appealed. The Court of Appeal held that the risk that the prosecution had to prove should be real as opposed to fanciful or hypothetical. In this case, there had been no previous accident and there was nothing wrong with the construction of the steps. There was no real risk of the kind contemplated by the 1974 Act and so the conviction was held to be unsafe. The appeal was allowed.	**HSWA** – 'Risk' must be real rather than fanciful or hypothetical.
R. v. Swan Hunter Shipbuilders Ltd (1982)	During the construction of "HMS Glasgow" at Tyneside, an oxygen valve was left open and a spark from the welding caused an intense fire to break out. Eight men were killed. Although the shipbuilders had distributed safety guidance to their own employees on the use of oxygen equipment, they had not done so to the subcontracted employees. Swan Hunter Ltd were prosecuted for failure to provide a safe system of work (**Health and Safety at Work, etc. Act 1974**, s.2).	Safe place of work. Provision of information.
Stark v. The Post Office (2000)	Stark was a postman and had been issued with a bicycle to help in deliveries. While riding the bicycle in connection with work, the front brake broke and he was thrown over the handlebars, sustaining a serious injury. The cause of the failure was held to be either metal fatigue or a manufacturing defect, neither of which would have been revealed on even the most "perfectly rigorous" inspection. It was nevertheless held that reg. 6(1) **PUWER** imposed an absolute duty on the Post Office to maintain the bicycle in an efficient state, in efficient working order and in good repair and that this had not been done. The Post Office were therefore found liable.	Absolute duty to maintain work equipment.

© RRC International

Case	Description	Subject Area
Summers v. Frost (1955)	Frost's thumb was trapped while operating a moving grinding wheel. The defendant argued that securing and fencing the machine would make the machine unusable. The court upheld breach of absolute duty.	Absolute duty.
Sutherland v. Hatton and Others (2002)	In this appeal case, brought by four employers in cases where damages had been awarded for work-related stress, the Court of Appeal set out some general principles to apply in such cases. The result of this case was to make it harder for employees to succeed in claims for work-related stress.	Employers' liability for work-related stress.
Uddin v. Associated Portland Cement Ltd (1965)	In trying to remove a pigeon in a factory, a machinery attendant climbed onto a platform then on a cabinet housing an unguarded revolving steel shaft. Although it was not foreseeable that an employee should climb onto the machine, it was held that a person forgetting to switch off the machine during maintenance was foreseeable and that the employers were in breach of the **Factories Act** whereby all employees should be protected.	Statutory duty. Contributory negligence.
Viasystems (Tyneside) Ltd v. Thermal Transfer (Northern) Ltd (2005)	Viasystems Ltd had engaged Thermal Transfer Ltd to install air conditioning in their factory. Thermal Transfer had subcontracted ducting work to S&P Darwell Ltd who had contracted with a third company, CAT Metalwork Services, to provide fitters and fitters' mates on a labour only basis. A fitter's mate supplied by CAT Metalwork, but under the supervision of a fitter contracted to S&P Darwell, negligently caused a flood. Viasystems sued all three contract companies for damages arising from the flood. It was held on appeal that dual vicarious liability was legally possible and that both S&P Darwell and CAT Metalwork Services were therefore found to be vicariously liable for the negligence.	Vicarious liability - two separate employers can be vicariously liable for negligence of a single employee.

Case	Description	Subject Area
Walker v. Northumberland County Council (1995)	W was employed as an area social services officer in an area with a high proportion of child-care problems. He suffered a nervous breakdown because of stress resulting from his high workload. On recovering, and before resuming work, it was agreed he would receive assistance in order to lessen his burden. He did not receive sufficient assistance and six months later suffered a second breakdown which forced him to cease work permanently. It was held that it was part of the employer's duty of care to provide a safe system of work. The employer chose to continue employing him, knowing he required additional effective help but did not provide effective help. It was reasonably foreseeable that in not providing the necessary assistance further psychiatric damage could occur. The judgment was in favour of the claimant.	Foreseeability - liability for work-related stress.
Wilsons and Clyde Coal Co. Ltd v. English (1938)	A miner was leaving the pit when the haulage plant was switched on, crushing him against the wall. The House of Lords (whose appellate role is now fulfilled by the Supreme Court) held that it was the personal duty of the employer to take reasonable care.	Employer's common law duty of care.